MEMORIES of a BABY BOOMER from MANSFIELD

MEMORIES of a BABY BOOMER from MANSFIELD

JOHN S. ADAMESCU

XULON PRESS

DEDICATION

To the memory of my mother, Ruth. For our long talks reminding me of the great times I had as a child growing up, and to all of the baby boomers out there that know the authenticity of a brisk winter day, playing in the crisp snow with all of the neighborhood kids.

ACKNOWLEDGMENT

This book is written in memory of my parents, Joseph and Ruth Adamescu. A thank you goes out to Gayle, Tim, Jim and Dayna, Emily, Sarah, and Pack for help with the pictures in my footnotes. It also goes out to my daughter Liz and my son Phil for their help in proofreading and setting the pages for me, and to my sons Steve and Chris for all their encouragement while writing the book.

MY FAMILY TREE
(Maternal)

Mueller—Mueller
    Catherine

Jud—Kleinhaus
    Paulina
    Martha (Mattie)
    Hulda

Philip Smith, Sr.—Catherine Mueller
    Peter
    William (Will)
    Jacob (Jake)
    Philip, Jr.

William Schettler—Paulina Jud
    Jeannette (Nettie)
    Theodore (Ted)
    Florence
    Paul
    Clara
    Charles (Charley)
    Marie
    Emma
    Frieda
    Herbert

Philip Smith, Jr.—Emma Schettler
    Paul
    Raymond (Ray)
    Ruth
    James (Jimmie)

Joseph Adamescu, Jr. —Ruth Smith
    John
    Susan
    Jeanne
    Timothy (Tim)
    James (Jimmy)
    Joseph, II (Joey) (d)
    Patrick (Pack)

John Adamescu — Gayle Wagner
    Stephen (Steve)
    Christopher (Chris)
    Philip (Phil)
    Elizabeth (Liz)

Chris Adamescu—DeYette Little
    Jannec (Nico)

Liz Adamescu—John Budion

MY FAMILY TREE
(Paternal)

<u>Paul N. Adamescu—Juken Petra</u>   <u>Miklos Berariu—??????</u>
   Paul N., Jr.   Mary M.
   Joseph B.
   John S., Sr.

<u>Joseph B. Adamescu—Mary M. Berariu</u>
    Paul N., II
    Joseph J.
    John S.

<u>Paul N. Adamescu—Rose Kimble</u>
    Catherine (Cathy)
    Paul N. (Nick), III
    Joseph (Joe)
    William (Bill)
    Thais (Ti)
    Michael (Mike)
    Philip (Phil)

<u>Joseph J. Adamescu, Jr.—Ruth Smith</u>
    John
    Susan
    Jeanne
    Timothy (Tim)
    James (Jimmy)
    Joseph, II (Joey)
    Patrick (Pack)

<u>John S. Adamescu—Grace Pederson</u>
    Carol
    Thomas (Tom)
    Dorothy
    Marilyn

Table of Contents

DEDICATION v
ACKNOWLEDGMENT vii
MY FAMILY TREE - Maternal viii
MY FAMILY TREE - Paternal ix

Chapter One—Streams of Thought 1
Chapter Two—Mansfield's Sesquicentennial 8
Chapter Three—Joe and Ruth Get Married 10
Chapter Four—Grandma Emma and Her Husbands 17
Chapter Five—Our New House 21
Chapter Six—A Merry Christmas Tree 25
Chapter Seven—A Litany of Neighborhood Children 28
Chapter Eight—Mixed Nicknames 31
Chapter Nine—Chicago Tenderfoot 33
Chapter Ten—Grandma Emma's Bakery 36
Chapter Eleven—My Sweet Godmother Dorothy 38
Chapter Twelve—Building an Outdoor Fireplace 44
Chapter Thirteen—Winter Time, Fun Time 48

Chapter Fourteen—The Old Baltimore &
    Ohio Railroad Tracks 59

Chapter Fifteen—Joseph and Mary Adamescu
    Come to America 64

Chapter Sixteen—Grandma Adamescu and Me 71

Chapter Seventeen—Grandpa Adamescu and Me 75

Chapter Eighteen—Summer Play 78

Chapter Nineteen —My Father's Call to
    5:00 AM Sunday Mass 80

Chapter Twenty—A New Shopping Center, Kindergarten,
    John Gets Lost 84

Chapter Twenty One—My Early St. Peters' Friends 89

Chapter Twenty-Two—Flying Kites,
    Catching Lightning Bugs 93

Chapter Twenty Three—Visits to Dr. Staker and
    Dr. Acomb 96

Chapter Twenty-Four—Favorite Toys 99

Chapter Twenty-Five—Stout's Grocery Market et. al. 102

Chapter Twenty-Six —Cindy Lou Who, and Other Pets 107

Chapter Twenty-Seven—Television, Our New
    Wonderful Gadget 110

Chapter Twenty-Eight—Our Family Automobile
    Early History 114

Chapter Twenty-Nine—My Father Bought
    Two Bikes for Me 117

Table of Contents

Chapter Thirty—The Beautiful Woods, Listening to Helen . . 120

Chapter Thirty-One—My Friend, Stanley Popp 123

Chapter Thirty-Two—Life Up at the Rusiska's New House . . 126

Chapter Thirty-Three—The Adamescu's Early Trip to
 Niagara Falls 128

Chapter Thirty-Four—The Woods, My First Big Treehouse,
 Learning a Lesson 131

Chapter Thirty-Five —John Learns Another Lesson,
 A Robot Attack From Next Door 135

Chapter Thirty-Six—Little Georgie Rusiska 138

Chapter Thirty-Seven—My Final Thoughts 140

EPILOGUE 143

BIOGRAPHY 145

Chapter One
Streams of Thought

12/12/2008

Today, my mother Ruth related to me that our maternal grandfather Philip's family originally lived in the Crestline, Ohio area, as his father (Philip, Sr.) worked for the railroad (Crestline was a thriving railroad center in those days). The story goes that he was an alcoholic and his wife, Catherine (Mueller), eventually left him, taking with her their five sons, and moved back to Mansfield, Ohio where the family settled, so that she would have family support in raising her children (the story of what happened to Philip, Sr. gets cloudy at this point). It is unclear whether or not the two of them ever reconciled or whether, as the "official" family story has it, he was killed by a train or perhaps died of tuberculosis. Needless to say, the five sons were raised without a father. Peter, the oldest of the Smith children, also took to the bottle somewhere along the way and he too died a tragic death. One night, in the dead of a Mansfield winter, he got roaring drunk and stumbled home to his mother's house on North Diamond Street.

The reason why is unclear, but he passed out and froze to death at the front door, unable to get into the house.

It also was interesting to find out that Great Grandmother Smith (Mueller) simply did not care at all for my Grandmother Emma (Schettler). When Grandfather Philip and

Emma and Philip, married, standing in front of their house

Grandmother Emma were first married, they lived with Great Grandmother Smith in her house on North Diamond Street in the "flats". After several less-than-cordial disagreements and crying fits due to this dislike, Grandmother Emma left Philip to move back to her mother and father's house on South Main Street. Grandfather Philip became distraught over losing his new bride so he too left his mother's house to again be with the "love of his life."

They eventually moved into a rented house at the corner of South Adams Street and Home Avenue (Home Avenue was named for the Mansfield Children's home, an orphanage, at the corner of Hedges Street and what was then known as Clay Street).

> The recent change from **Clay Street** in the fourth ward, to **Home Avenue**, was deemed necessary as there were two Clay Streets in the city. Home Avenue was considered more appropriate for the one in the fourth ward, as it leads direct from Diamond Street to the Children's Home and the change was made accordingly.
>
> The more recent rechristening of **Water Street** proves the facts above stated. Why it was ever named Water Street is a question to be asked in vain unless it was merely to give the street a name for there is no body of water from which it could derive the name. It will be some time before Mansfielders will forget to call it by its original name and this was one of the arguments offered in favor of the change for when it shall become familiarly known as **Adams Street** (named after John Adams, the second President

Details of Mansfield, Ohio street names

In time, Philip and Emma built their own house next door to the rental (east) in 1924 at 126 Home Avenue. This is where Grandma Emma raised her family, buried her husband(s) and lived there until 1975. She then moved out to the west side of town to a house on Harvard Avenue, across the street from her daughter Ruth and her family, where she lived until her death in 1990 at 94 years of age.

Grandma Emma when she was 18 years old

Another interesting fact is that Great Grandmother Smith (Mueller), and her sons, Philip, Jake, and Ed eventually all had houses on the same block. The boundaries of which were Home Avenue on the north (Philip), Dale Avenue on the south (Great

Grandmother Smith and Jake), and South Adams Street on the west (Ed). The only exception was their brother Will, who lived in the North End on Newman Street. Now, that's what I call family unity!

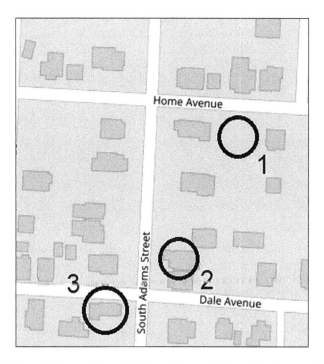

Map of Home, Dale and South Adams Street. 1) Grandma Emma's house 2) Great Uncle Ed's house 3) Grandpa Adamescu's house

My mother Ruth's cousin (and best buddy), Esther Leopold (Great Aunt Clara's daughter), grew up on the south side of Mansfield on Greenwood Avenue west of South Main Street. Mom also thought that Helen Moore (Rusiska) grew up not far from Esther on the south side of Hammond Avenue east of South Main Street (it was near the old fire station). I remember that Ken and Della Grembling lived on the southside of Greenwood Avenue, not far from Clara and Esther's house. They had a daughter, Dorothy, who was in my sister Jeanne's class in grade school at St Peter's Elementary. The Gremblings were friends of my Dad, who worked with Ken on construction jobs (Ken was a stonemason). His wife, Della, became an entrepreneur and opened a restaurant on Rt. 42 south of Mansfield in the mid-'50s. She enlisted my Dads help in the marketing of the new restaurant. My father designed and built a large roadside sign made of plywood in the shape of a teakettle for Della, which she installed in front of her restaurant on Rt. 42. The "inspiration" for this design came to my Dad from an old tea kettle that had been rattling around our basement at home ever since I could remember. I still remember my Dad (I was 6 or 7 years old at the time) making a template for the design by placing the teakettle in front of him and sketching its outline on a scrap of 1/4" plywood (my Dad had a real knack for drawing). He then cut out the design and transferred it to two pieces (front and back) of 3/4" plywood to make the finished sign. I don't remember if he had anything to do with the final painting of the sign, but I do remember seeing the sign in place on Rt. 42 the one time he took me to Della's restaurant for a hamburger and french fries on a cool sunny day in the fall!! Ken also supplied and installed the flagstone walkway which wended its way from our breezeway to the end of our lot near the woods.

Dad hanging baby clothes on the clothesline on our walkway, around 1950

Chapter Two
Mansfield's Sesquicentennial

12/13/2008

I remember, in 1958, Mansfield was celebrating its sesquicentennial (150) years in existence. I was 8 or 9 years old at the time. I don't remember too much about the event except the members of Carpenters Local 735 (my Dad was a loyal member) all grew beards for the occasion. My Dad had a picture of all the carpenters in coats and bowties resplendent in all their beards!

They called themselves "The Brothers of the Brush". I also recall that the beard irritated my Dad's face (it itched) and he was always threatening to shave it off. He did, but not until after the celebration was over. I do vaguely remember standing on the north side of Park Avenue West near Weldon Avenue and watching the Sesquicentennial parade pass by with my Mom and siblings. The parade included many floats which represented various community businesses and organizations.

Mansfield's Sesquicentennial

The officers of Local 735 in Mansfield, Ohio resplendent in their sport coats, bowties and beards.

The carpenters had built a float showing the growth of Mansfield over the past 150 years. They had constructed a miniature log cabin and a "modern" house that rode upon their float. After the parade, the carpenters gave the modern house to us Adamescu kids (probably because there were so many of us) but it was delivered to our driveway with the roof sawn off (no doubt to make it easier to transport in a pickup truck). However, this rendered the house useless to play in, as the roof would eventually slide off causing my Mom to declare it off-limits. My Mom wanted us kids to get the log cabin, but that went to the Miles kids (they also had a large family). We played in the house, minus the roof, for the remainder of 1958, but it didn't survive the winter and disappeared into the "dustbin" of history (not unlike many other things which we kids inherited).

Chapter Three
Joe and Ruth Get Married

12/30/2008

After my parents were married on Valentine's Day in February of 1947, they spent their honeymoon in Niagara Falls, NY. They traveled up to the Falls in their brand new, beautiful 1947 Pontiac Streamliner.

My Mom and Dad sitting on the fender of the Pontiac on their honeymoon

Joe and Ruth Get Married

When they returned from their honeymoon, they lived for a time with my Grandmother Emma at her house on Home Avenue. This was after my Grandfather Philip was killed in 1940 in an electrical accident at the Walpark Building near the Leland Hotel. He was an electrician working for the Richland Electric Company and he and another man were working on one of the elevators in the building. He was underneath the elevator and was killed instantly when he came in contact with a 220V wire and was unable to move in such a small space. He was a two-time member of the City Council in Mansfield. He was also considered one of Mansfield's outstanding youth leaders and gave freely of his time to them. He was the district Boy Scout commissioner and he received the Silver Eagle award as well as the veteran award in recognition of his 15 years as a scoutmaster. All in all, he was a great man.

Memories of a Baby Boomer from Mansfield

Civic Leader Killed By Current as He Works on Elevator Motor.

Stunned by his unexpected death, Mansfielders in all walks of life today mourned the passing of Philip Smith, 46, of 54 Home avenue, Mansfield city councilman who was electrocuted yesterday in a downtown office building.

Smith, an electrician, was working on the electrical equipment of the elevators in the Walpark building. He came in contact with a 220-volt wire, grounding the current and was killed instantly. The accident occurred in the elevator motor house on the roof of the building. With him at the time was Howard Daubenspeck, 105 West Fifth street, with whom he had worked the past 18 years. Both were employed by the Richland Electric company. Smith was the oldest employe of the firm, having worked for the company 28 years.

Hearing Smith groan while working in the small compartment, Daubenspeck threw the electric switch shutting off the current and ran to the floor below to summon help.

Dr. Charles L. Shaler, whose offices are on the fifth floor, rushed to the roof of the building. Patrolman George Yoakum summoned from the street, immediately

(Continued on Page 10, Col. 8)

INDEPENDENT FOR SENATE

COLUMBUS — (UP) — H. K. Tekla of Cleveland asked the secretary of state's office today for nominating petitions to qualify as an independent candidate for U. S. senator at the Nov. 5 election. He would need 25,000 signatures to file.

2 Starts Job

PHILIP SMITH

MEETING OFF

Councilman's Death Postpones Study of W. Fourth Puzzle.

A special meeting of city council scheduled for tonight was postponed today due to the unexpected death of Philip Smith, Democratic councilman-at-large.

Mayor William J. Locke had issued the call for the special session yesterday to pass on legislation that would permit the state to proceed with the West Fourth street improvement.

Locke said he had rescinded the order today and that Council Clerk William J. Beer, jr., had been instructed to notify council members of the action.

He said he expected that council would be called sometime next week to consider the proposal, turned down at the May 7 meeting. Early action was necessary in order that the state can get the paving project under way.

---

term as councilman-at-large Jan. 1, having been elected to the office last fall. He was a Democrat.

As a member of council, he was chairman of the newly created traffic committee and was working with the Citizens' Traffic committee on the Mansfield traffic problem. He was also chairman of the parks committee and a member of the sewer committees.

Mr. Smith was probably one of Mansfield's outstanding youth leaders and gave freely of his time to them.

As Mansfield district Boy Scout commissioner, he was recently given the Silver Beaver award, made annually by the Boy Scouts for outstanding service to boyhood.

In addition to that award, Smith also received a veteran award in recognition of his 13 years as a scoutmaster. He first became active in the movement in 1924 as a committeeman of troop No. 5 at Hedges school. He was scoutmaster from 1930 to 1931, when he was appointed district commissioner.

Mr. Smith was the first chairman of the city recreation board, an office he held from 1924 to 1937.

A member of the St. John's Evangelical church and Sunday school, he taught the Bracca class for the past 20 years. He was a member of the church council and brotherhood and was former president of the council.

He was active in Hedges park community movements and was a former president of the Hedges school Parent-Teachers association. He was a member of the Order of the Owls and the I. O. O. F., serving on the board of trustees of the latter organization.

Mr. Smith is survived by his wife, Emma; three sons, Paul, Raymond and James, and a daughter, Ruth, all at home; two brothers, Edward and William Smith, both of Mansfield.

His body was removed to the Wappner funeral home where services will be held at 1:30 p. m. Saturday. Rev. Paul H. Saleste, pastor of the St. John's Evangelical church will officiate. Burial will be in Mansfield cemetery.

My Grandfather Philip's obituary

During this time (and before the children), Mom worked at Mansfield General Hospital on Glessner Avenue as a Registered Nurse and Dad worked at Mansfield Tire and Rubber as a tire builder. Eventually, Dad decided that he would rather be a carpenter, so he left The Tire and went to work for Bill Auer, a contractor. One of the first jobs my Dad worked on was at the far end of Mansfield, right at the city limits. Bill Auer was the original developer along with Laser & Walker, of the Harvard/Grasmere/Westgate development. It was here that Mom and Dad decided to build their first house at 78 Harvard Avenue (the address eventually changed to its current number, 76, when Bob and Carol McLaughlin purchased the half-lot to the north from my parents in order to build their house on that site). The McLaughlins' address became 68 Harvard Avenue. Our house was the first new house built on the street. Harvard, Grasmere, and Westgate were originally "dead-end" streets. Each street terminated into Park Avenue West to the north (except for Harvard Avenue which jogged east onto Tudor Street and then continued north at "Harvard Extension", to Park Avenue West) and into the Draffen/Black Estates (a farm) on the south end (Mr. Black was the CEO of Mansfield General Hospital). The farm fields were normally planted with either corn or soybeans or, occasionally, left fallow. These fields were always one of many sources of great adventure for my friends and me back then!

The first house on Harvard Avenue belonged to Augustus (Gus) and Bertha Schroeder. Their house was on the west side of the street and was constructed of brick in the 1920s style. It had sat there alone for the first 22 years of existence. They had two daughters, Miriam and Esther. I can't imagine the wonderful times they had in the woods behind their house with their Dad taking them along on his forays back there!

One of the single greatest things about our new home location on Harvard Avenue was the "woods" which ran the entire length of our street from PAW (Park Avenue West) on the north and on up through the Draffen/Black Estate on the south. Part of a long ago abandoned farm, they were rich in mystery and diversity with deep gullies, streams, a myriad of old trails, which my Mom told me must have been made by Indians who lived there a long time ago, and mysterious names carved into the older, larger trees.

I later found out that the trails were made by Mr. Schroeder, but as a child, there were Indians about!! Behind the woods, there was a short line B&O (Baltimore & Ohio) railroad track that ran from Sandusky, Ohio in the north down to Butler, Ohio at its southern terminus.

Joe and Ruth Get Married

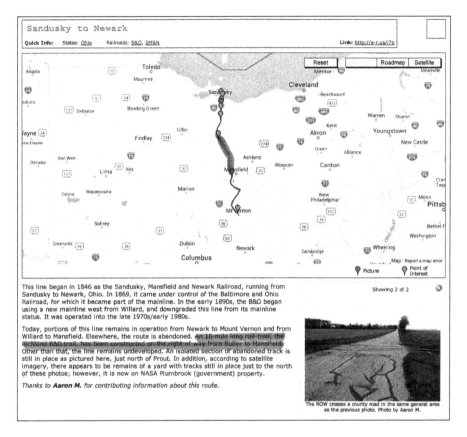

Sandusky to Mt. Gilead Railroad Spur which ran behind our house

Just beyond the tracks, to the west, ran Touby's Run, a creek that would swell into a river each year as the winter snows would melt. Both of these also added to the wonderful adventures we had as children.

One year, in December, my friend from across the street, Danny Maglott who was a year or two older than me, received a CO2 powered BB gun for Christmas! I was over at his house and we decided to try it back in the woods. The temperature was hovering right around freezing and it had snowed pretty heavily that

Christmas, so we had all the making for a great adventure! We trudged back into the woods and had a wonderful time wading through snow drifts and shooting his BB gun at the occasional bird (don't worry folks no actual birds were harmed in this adventure). We checked out all the creeks and discovered some of them were frozen, but some were not. We did however both managed to get our boots full of water, but that hardly kept us from having a great time! Since the snow was so deep, we quickly became tired of walking through the woods, so we went back to Danny's house and played, in the warmth and comfort of his parent's living room, with all the toys he had received that year from Santa!

Chapter Four
Grandma Emma and Her Husbands

01/20/2009

My Grandma Emma, bless her soul, was married three times in her 94 years of life and she outlived all of her husbands. Her first husband was Philip Smith, my Grandfather, who as previously mentioned, was electrocuted in 1940 while at work on an elevator in the old Walpark Building. My Mothers' cousin Esther wrote a very touching poem for my Grandfather Philip after his death and my Mom had it hanging on her wall until the day she died in 2013.

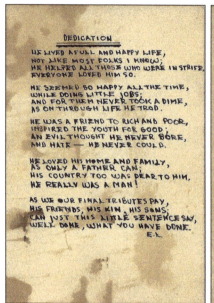 

Esther's poem dedicated to Grandpa Philip, my Mom's father

Esther was 18 years old. My Grandma's second husband was a simple man named Jimmie Sellers. He and Grandma Emma were married somewhere around 1950 or so, and I didn't get to know much about him. I don't remember anything other than one night as I was visiting my Grandma Emma, he walked through the darkened dining room of her house and into the kitchen where Grandma and I were sitting at the kitchen table. He held out to me a small wooden birdhouse that he had made! It was painted white and had a gable roof covered with heavy tar paper. At my excited request, he sketched a picture of a little bird on it in pencil above the round cutout opening in front.

That little birdhouse found a place of honor in a branch of the pink dogwood tree that used to grow behind our garage on Harvard Avenue. It was a small tree and I was able to climb into it anytime I wanted to visit my little treasure. A small group of wrens made a home of it sometime later! I don't have any other recollections of Jimmie Sellers other than this one time. I must have met him at some point, but I can't remember the place. I was told that he worked in a machine shop and that he was crushed by a piece of machinery that had hit him in the chest. He died not long after that. He and Grandma were married for only a very short amount of time. Her third and last husband was a very nice, but simple, gentleman named Oscar Spell. Grandma Emma and he were married in 1956. Oscar lived until 1969 when he died of a massive heart attack while working at Mansfield General Hospital. Originally, Oscar was an oilman on the Pennsylvania Railroad. He worked on the old steam locomotives, in Crestline, Ohio (which was also his hometown), for many years until the Pennsylvania railroad shut down its operations in Crestline sometime in the very early 1960s. This event directly coincided with the advent and large-scale use of more powerful and efficient diesel locomotives...ah, "progress"!

 The first time I met Oscar, Grandma and he had just begun to date and she had invited him over to her house on Home Avenue. My sister, Susan, and I were up visiting Grandma Emma when Oscar pulled up in his 1953 Oldsmobile Rocket 88! It was a beautiful two-tone blue and white car! However, because Oscar was very shy (or so we found out) he refused to get out of his car because Susan and I were there. I don't quite remember, but I recollected that Grandma was not able to talk him into staying and she was somewhat unhappy that he had acted this way. The most interesting fact that I have taken away from this period in Grandma Emma's life was that she always met and married men who met her standards, which were very high. It was also an interesting fact that she never had to change the monogram on her bath towels, as each of her husband's last names began with the letter "S"!

Chapter Five
Our New House

03/10/2009

I don't remember anything of the wet and muddy streets my Mom and Dad endured as our house neared completion in 1949/50, remember, it was the first new house built on Harvard Avenue. My first recollections, when I was 4 or 5, were of Harvard Avenue being a place of beautiful lawns, early and mature growth trees, and houses that were all neatly manicured and painted and, of course, there were kids everywhere!! At the bottom of Harvard Avenue was a deep gully next to the Timan's house, which served as the catch basin for the stormwater runoff from the streets in our development. There was a very large (42") concrete pipe that extended out from the hill at the bottom of the gully that connected all the storm drains on the street, the runoff from which then emptied into a shallow pool that formed in the ground at the front of the pipe. This pool and the surrounding hill became one of our most exciting places, as small boys, to explore and play, much to the dismay of our mothers! As small children, the hill was Mt. Everest, the pool was like a great ocean, and the woods were just like Sherwood Forest! One of my friends even had the courage (Danny Maglott) to climb into the storm drain and follow it (through the pipe when it was dry outside), underground, back up Harvard Avenue where those of us who weren't courageous (but perhaps more intelligent-yours truly) looked "down" in awe at the brave soul who looked "up" at us from under the drain gate in the road in front of Marston's house more than 200 feet away from the gully!! I'll never forget the smell that emanated from that storm drain. It was a clean but musty odor of moisture that wasn't at all offensive but was certainly different and memorable. The inside of the drain pipe was always much cooler than the day's temperature, even in the height of summer. At the top of the hill, closest to the gray apartment building on Tudor Street and at the edge of the gravel driveway at the back under the apartments, we had discovered a very cozy "cave" on the side of the hill running down into the gully. It was no doubt formed by bulldozers when the construction workers backfilled and leveled the ground near the gully, but to us, it was a cavern! Eventually, the rain and ensuing settling of the ground filled our cave, but we enjoyed it for at least one or two more summers! When we got a little older, Danny Maglott and I used to "gig" frogs in the pool (on second thought, he "gigged" them and I watched).

Another story about Danny Maglott was when we were younger, we all played in the neighborhood in the yards of one another. One night during the summer, Danny, along with Jeff Bechtel, George Rusiska, Joe Henny, and us youngsters, were playing in Danny's front yard. They were doing "amazing" things to try and impress us young ones as Danny came up with a great idea! They would throw a pop bottle up into the air and then try to catch it! Well, all went along smoothly, although rather dangerously, until it was Danny's turn to catch the bottle. Then it turned dangerous. You see, Danny wasn't as skilled as his three cohorts and when he threw the pop bottle up, it did 3 or 4 revolutions, then it came down. Now, let me interject here. Danny's Dad and his mother Coretta were in their living room, probably watching the news or something worthwhile, when out the front door they heard a terrible scream followed by a bunch of words they most probably wouldn't like to hear. Danny had missed catching the bottle, and it came down on one of his big, beautiful front teeth…and broke off a chip of his tooth. Needless to say, when they rushed out their front door and saw Danny holding his mouth, rather painfully, they were a mixture of worried and angry. After this, throwing pop bottles up in the air was totally forbidden and Danny had a chipped tooth for years so that he could show people!

Another wonderful adventure that presented itself to us kids, mostly the boys, was the "monkey vines" which grew in abundance back in the woods. Some very good vines grew on the sides of the hills and ravines that meandered throughout the trees. Some of the older boys in the neighborhood including Jimmy Santoro, Joe Henney, George Rusiska, and Jeff Bechtel, were able to prune the vines so that we could swing out over the abyss on them. Truth be told, this was probably the most dangerous thing we kids did, and it eventually caused much consternation and worry for our parents, mostly for our moms. The one that is most vivid in my memory was the huge vine that swung out over the hill behind Jimmy Santoro's house. The hill must have dropped 75 feet to the gully at the bottom! Even the older boys began to refuse us use of the vines, as they too began to see how dangerous it was. Eventually, Jimmy's dad, Joe Santoro cut the vine down, which no doubt saved a couple of trips to the emergency room. After this we were constantly on the lookout for the next great "monkey vine", but we never found one that came nearly as close to being as much fun. Although, a few years later, Ken Holt, the older brother of Gary Holt (they moved into the Hericks' house when they moved around 1957), found a vine that was a close second to the Santoro vine in the woods behind their house, which proved to be pretty thrilling as well. Unfortunately, that vine also met its demise when my friend Mike Miller fell off it while no one else was around and broke his collarbone. Luckily, he was able to make it on his own back to his house on Trimble Road, where his parents took him to the emergency room, where he had a cast placed on his injured shoulder. Ken Holt cut that vine down the very next day upon stern instruction from his Father!

Chapter Six
A Merry Christmas Tree

01/10/09

Growing up, we never had much money. From time to time this bothered me although I don't remember that it ever weighed heavily on my psyche. We were monetarily poor which was especially prominent when the weather turned cold and blustery. My Dad was a carpenter and belonged to the local carpenters union (Local 735). Because of the weather, construction work in our part of the country was often ground to a halt. He would take the occasional "inside" job when available, but that was very rarely. Being a staunch union man, Dad would never take work that was non-union. Because of this, my Dad's proclivity to fight non-union work, and the fact that Mom and Dad had seven of us kids, we were never able to buy "luxuries". Keep in mind that our "luxuries" would no doubt have been considered everyday purchases to most of our friends. One Christmas, when I was 12 or 13, "luxury" came to include our family Christmas tree. By this time, contractor Gus Sloboda had begun work at the top of the street on his new housing development which was called, "Ballylin". The Draffens had finally sold off the farm to Gus, with the stipulation that it be named after Mr. Draffen's ancestral family home in Ireland. What had once been a magical cornfield/playground was quickly being transformed into an extension of the Harvard/Grasmere/Westgate development with higher-priced new housing being built. There were, however, some remnants of that beautiful property still in place that winter. There was a stand of the prettiest evergreen trees, which stood near the woods on the west side of the old cornfield.

Our family property with the woods behind

By this time, I had decided that there was no way I could allow my brothers and sisters to go without a Christmas tree. I made up my mind that I would get one of those trees if I had the chance. One snowy winter day, before Christmas, I trekked up the street into the new development, through the now-frozen mud, and into the stand of evergreens. I had taken one of my Dad's hand saws with me. I picked out the prettiest tree that I felt would fit into our living room (I was always a pragmatist) and proceeded to cut it down. The trip home would have to be via a more clandestine route as I didn't know if I was breaking some law or not and I couldn't take the tree straight down the street. I decided to drag the tree back down to our house at the bottom of the street, but this time I would go through the woods to avoid any detection. As I struggled over hills and gullies and through brambles, I suddenly discovered that there wasn't anything quite as quiet and beautiful as a forest of trees when it had been snowing! The freshly fallen snow crunched under my feet as I walked. It was very quiet in the woods with the snow falling softly, the day dimming to dusk as I headed home with my prize. I managed to maneuver the tree through the forest and when I successfully reached our backyard, I felt like I had just conquered Mount Everest. I was so happy!! That year we all said that we had the prettiest tree on the street!

Chapter Seven
A Litany of Neighborhood Children

01/17/2009

One of the nicest things about our neighborhood, when we were young, was the fact that there were always a lot of kids, approximately the same age, to play with. This was right after World War II, and the baby boom was in full bloom! If you happened to be fighting with or had a disagreement with one friend, you could always find another to hang around with. My Mom always commented on the fact that there were, at some point, 70-75 children on our little dead-end street! I don't know when she took her count, but I do remember the following, starting at the northwest end of Harvard Avenue next to the gully (these were the original owners of the houses on our street):

Name:Number of Children:	
Rose and Patty Timan	2
Jimmy and Mary Jo Santoro	2
The McLaughlin Girls	3

A Litany of Neighborhood Children

The Adamescu Kids	7
George, Kenny and Bobby Rusiska	3
The Schnug Kids	3
Tim and Chrissy Herrick	2
Robbie and Debbie Line	2
Nancy, Curt and Davy Wycoff	3
Allen and Jeff Bechtel	2
Ricky and Rita Mohr	2
Jackie and Debby Miller	2
Scott Gilbert	1
Mark, Dennis and Bruce Luedy	3
Barbara Lashey	1
Gary, Robin and Joey Jakubick	3
The Benzin Girls	2
The McKinley Girls	2
Kathy, Kevin and Dorothy Wires	3
Sheri Wilson (the "starlet")	1
Linda Smith	1
Karl and Dennis Schwechheimer	2
Vic Kuhn	1

Kay and Danny Maglott	2
Gaileen, Stan and Joy Popp	3
The Theaker Kids	4
Tommy Dahl	1
Susie Adomatis	1
Peaches (Nicole), Ginger and Chris Marston	3
John and Joe Henney	2
TOTAL	69

WOW!!

Chapter Eight

Mixed Nicknames

01/20/2009

My Mom had seven kids and thus, could not be faulted for sometimes forgetting which one of us she was yelling at! She often went through the litany of our names before hitting on the correct combination: "Tim, Jim, Joe–Pack!!" Another of her favorite sayings was fairly religious in tone: "Jesus, Mary and Joseph!! What happened now?!!" She was also quite prolific in giving each of us an "endearing" nickname: I was "Johnny Bonnie", Susan was "Sootie Bootles", Jeanne became "Jeanne, Jeanne Jelly Beanie". Tim had a couple: "Timtoe, Simento, Pimento" was from Mom (Mom always had Tim pegged as her future sainted priest because of his early kindness, especially to animals), and "Professor Winkle Dinkle" was from me. Jimmie was "Jamie McPheeters", Joey was "Hoss" (from the "Bonanza" TV show) because of his large size at birth and Patrick was, for a while, "Pookie" and then "Packy" (shortened from "pachyderm" for a baby elephant) but the nickname that stuck was "Pack," which is how he is known today. My Dad was not one for nicknames, but he did come up with a few that were memorable. As what so often happens in families, after Grandpa Adamescu passed away in 1960, Dad and his brothers had a falling out. For many years afterward, the three of them didn't speak to each other and Dad came to refer to his brother Paul as the "Rat" and his brother John as the "Weasel". They reconciled around 1968. Ah, those were the days...

Chapter Nine

Chicago Tenderfoot

01/30/09

When she was older, Grandma Emma would occasionally regale us with tales of her youth. Out of these tales I came to realize that Grandma Emma, in her youth, tended to be an independent "little stinker" and also had a mind of her own. These were wonderful traits, but hardly ever seen in a young lady of her era. One of these tales revolved around her mother, Paulina's, brother, Tafey Jud and his family. Grandma Emma in her late 80s still gleefully recalled the tale of "Chicago Tenderfoot". I still remember Grandma Emma laughing so loud during the retelling of this story, that she had tears in her eyes! It seems that her Uncle Tafey moved to Chicago from Mansfield and settled there with his wife and children. During the summers when Grandma Emma was 12 or 13 she and her older sister, Clara, were required to go to Chicago and effectively become "handmaidens" to Uncle Tafey and his brood. She and Clara were paid the sum of $1.00 per week for their services. This may or may not have been as small a sum as it seems: remember this was 1907-08 and a good weekly wage was $10-15 a week! But to

Grandma Emma, the money wasn't the problem, it was that she somewhat resented having to give up a part of her summers in Mansfield on her family farm away from her friends and family and become indentured servants for her "snooty" cousins and their family in Chicago. She also resented what she viewed as their "holier than thou" demeanor towards Clara and herself. Now, Clara was not so independent nor a "stinker" nor did she exhibit a strong will of her own. So she resigned herself to her lot in Chicago and did her job as required. She even took advantage of a secretarial school there and learned to be a stenographer! But not Grandma Emma. No, she was not the "good soldier type". She put her foot down and refused to go to Chicago during the summers anymore! And she won! Now, you might wonder why I consider my dear Grandma Emma a "little stinker".

The proof of my theory comes from the tales of what she did, in particular, to her cousins from Chicago when they "graced" the Schettler farm in Mansfield with their "royal" presence during the summer. Grandma Emma and her siblings, growing up on the farm, went barefoot most of the time during the summer months. Because of this, the soles of their feet tended to take on a tough, leather-like texture, almost like wearing shoes. Grandma Emma had in mind that payback was hers for having to put up with Uncle Tafey and his offspring while in Chicago. The Lord may have said "revengeth is mine", but Grandma Emma had her own take on sweet retribution. Whenever any of the Jud cousins came to the farm for the first time, she had them take off their shoes as a fun thing to do and run with her through the cornfields that had been harvested. This meant corn stalk "stubble" was everywhere. This may have sounded like good fun to the "city slickers", but have you ever run barefoot through the cornfields after the harvest? Neither would the Jud cousins again after their first visit to the farm! This then was the story of "Chicago Tenderfoot"... I rest my case.

Chapter Ten
Grandma Emma's Bakery

02/12/2009

As a child, one of the best and most anticipated times was getting to sleep over at Grandma Emma's house on Home Avenue. There was a quiet calm about her house that made me feel protected and that all was right with the world. Often, when staying at her house, she would be busily involved in some sort of baking project (which was one of her finest skills) and, of course, I would get to sample her wares! As I sat in her living room I could hear the "tick, tick ticking" of the timer on her old Maytag gas stove and the sharp "ding" of the timer when the rolls or pies were done baking. Grandma always used lard in her baking, and I'm certain this is why her pastries were so flakey and delicious. She kept a five-gallon tin of lard on her back porch, which was always unheated. In the summer, the lard would be almost a semi-liquid consistency and in the winter, it was always mostly solid. Upon entering the dining room, my nose would pick up the wonderful smells of the bakery mixed with the faintest smell of sulfur and natural gas left over from when she lit the Tappen oven. Then, when I arrived in the kitchen, the smells collided with the warmth of the oven which enveloped me with a big "hug"! A very homey feeling would put me immediately at ease. During the holidays, both Grandma Emma and (Great) Aunt Nettie, if she was in town, would come out to our house on Harvard Avenue and bake up a Christmas cookie storm with my Mom! Christmas cutout butter cookies were always my favorite. It was so much fun helping to put the sprinkles and "jimmies" on them! Aunt Netties' claim to baking fame was her excellent recipe for old-fashioned, spicy, German Lebkuchen cookies, which no doubt she learned to make while at home as a child on the family farm at her mother Paulina's apron strings. I remember that after they were cooled, Mom would place them in a large tin can covered with layers of waxed paper and store them in the cool basement. She told me this was to keep them cool and soft. I really enjoyed those cookies and we never had them again after sweet Aunt Nettie passed away in the late 1960s. At home, during the rest of the year, my favorite cookie was a molasses crisp. I still like them to this day, although, I will admit, not too many of my family like them as much as I do. This is fine as there will always be more for me! My Mom was also "famous", at least to our next-door neighbor Helen Rusiska, for her meringue filling for pies. For some reason, Mom's meringue always came out fluffy, with just the right amount of stiffness, so she would occasionally be asked to make a couple of pies for Helen when she was entertaining. Mom could make both butterscotch and lemon meringue pies and either one was fine with me!

Chapter Eleven
My Sweet Godmother Dorothy

02/15/09

When I was a very young child one of the nicest things that happened to me, at least twice a year, was the card and present I would receive from my Godmother Dorothy Avery. She lived with her family in North Collins, NY. She and her husband George owned a small but profitable variety/grocery store in the area. "Dottie" was a dear Navy friend of my Mom, and when I was born, in 1949, she was asked to be my Godmother and Maurice Buzzard, who was a good friend of my Dad, was asked to be my Godfather.

Mom and Dottie (Case) Avery met while at the US Navy Nurses boot camp in upstate New York (Mom recollects it was called Fort Samson) along with another nurse, Jeanne Krickenberger (supposedly, my sister Jeanne was named after her). They spent six months there together and all became fast, lifelong friends.

My Sweet Godmother Dorothy

Map of North Collins, NY

They all ended up serving together after basic training at the Naval Air Station on North Island, California. Since they were Registered Nurses, they were also officers with the designation of Lt. JG (Lieutenant Junior Grade). This allowed them to "rub elbows" with the doctors and other assorted officers during WWII. My Mom always said wistfully, that those were the best days of her life. Dottie was the best and sweetest Godmother a small boy could ask for! She never forgot my birthday and occasionally would throw in another holiday card and gift for me each year. I don't remember much about the various gifts I received, but I do recall one of them very well! I was probably about 4 or 5 years old and I received a little cloth book from her about how a young man should groom himself. I especially remember that it had a page with a quarter of a saddle shoe on it that I could practice tying my shoe strings and another page had a little green comb and an attached mirror to practice combing my hair (which went unused as my Dad always had me in the shortest butch haircut)! I always looked forward to these times because she would also usually write me a short letter of encouragement along with the gift. I think this is how I got to realize what type of fine person Dottie was.

My Mom tells the story of how, after they were friends for a while, Dottie came to her one day with an obvious concern in her voice and told my Mom that she might not want to be friends with her anymore! Incredulous! My Mom asked her what on earth she could mean!! Dottie then told her that she was adopted. My Mom laughed and asked Dottie why she would think that this fact could ever change their friendship?! They remained close friends until Dottie passed away in 2002. After my wife, Gayle, and I were married in 1979, we drove to Cape Cod in Massachusetts for our honeymoon. I hadn't seen Dottie since she and George had come to my high school graduation in 1967. Actually, other than at my baptism, that was the only other time I had met them in person! On the way back to Cleveland from Cape Cod, I discovered that Interstate 90 passes only about 30 miles north of North Collins, NY (Dorothy's home). I told Gayle the story of my sweet Godmother Dottie, and she graciously agreed that we should stop and surprise them with a visit. We pulled into North Collins, which, by the way, isn't so much a city as it is a sprawling amalgamation of pretty homes and farms spread out over quite a large area. We didn't know where to begin to look for their house, but I did remember that they had a store.

My Sweet Godmother Dorothy

My Godmother Dorothy and my Godfather Maurice holding me after my baptism

We drove around until we found what looked like a variety/grocery store and we stopped in and inquired about George and Dorothy. We had stumbled into the right place! It wasn't really a store in the true sense of the word, as much as it was a large refurbished barn. Dottie and George weren't in the store at the time, but an employee phoned them for us and they invited us over for supper! Dorothy was so happy to see us, we had a wonderful dinner with George, Dottie, and their children!

Like a lot of wonderful stories, they sometimes don't have a happy ending. Dorothy's, unfortunately, was one of them. The last time I saw Dottie, I was working as the Director of Sales and Marketing for Gratry & Company, a boutique money management firm in Cleveland, Ohio. Part of my position required me to travel to different cities and states and call on various financial firms to sell our portfolio management to them. On one trip, I believe that it was in 1999 or 2000, I was traveling from Rochester, NY back to Buffalo, NY and for some unknown reason, I again noticed North Collins on the Rand McNally Atlas I was using for directions. Now, during that time, my Mom had informed me that Dottie's husband George had suffered a stroke and that she was struggling to keep the store open. I decided that, once again, I would surprise them with a visit. My timing could not have been worse. I called for information to find Dottie's telephone number and gave her a call. She wasn't at home, but her daughter Stephanie answered the phone and told me that Dottie would want to see me and that she would try to locate her. Stephanie gave me directions to her house, which I later discovered was a rental, as they had to sell their house to make ends meet. I was surprised at how different this house was from the one Gayle and I had visited in 1979. I arrived and was invited in by Stephanie and her aunt. To my chagrin, there was George, in the front room lying in a hospital bed. He was unable to move or speak and the feeling that I shouldn't be there immediately overwhelmed me. I somehow knew this wasn't how Dottie would have wanted me to see them. When she arrived home, I could see the horror in her eyes that I had come. She tried to act as though things were as they were in the past, but in my heart, I knew she was completely heartbroken. Dottie passed away in 2002, no doubt, in no small measure, from a broken heart. God bless my wonderful Godmother Dorothy.

Chapter Twelve
Building an Outdoor Fireplace

03/17/2009

When the Rusiskas' lived next to us at 84 Harvard Avenue, sometime in late 1953 or 1954, George Rusiska and my Dad built a "thank you" brick barbecue fireplace in our backyard very near the woods. These outdoor cooking grills and patios were all the rage in the 1950s! George was a masonry contractor and had been thankful for the use of Mom and Dad's telephone during the building of our development (it was the only one available on the street). George supplied the materials, gratis, and our Dad supplied the help. I remember that it was a sunny day and that it was somewhat cool outside as we were wearing our coats. After George had finished pouring the simple concrete foundation slab for our fireplace and it was "setting" up, his son, my friend Kenny, and my dog, Sparky, walked through the fresh concrete, thus memorializing their little footprints in history.

Building an Outdoor Fireplace

Picture of the brick fireplace in our backyard

Due to the ravages of time and neglect, the fireplace is long gone, but the footprints are still visible in the concrete pad that remains in the backyard, by the woods, to this day. I don't remember using the fireplace much for its intended purpose, as we didn't have a lot of family cookouts back then. We used it mostly for burning trash which was still permitted at the time, especially as our lot was at the farthest western boundaries of the city. However, when my friends or I would have a sleep out in the backyard, which we did somewhat frequently, we would cook hotdogs and roast marshmallows on the barbecue grill.

Another memory of my Dad and George was on a late spring day when I was around four or five, they took me and Kenny back into the woods with fishing poles to a spot that is still lovingly burned into my memory. There was a stream that ran down from the south and pooled in a small pond almost directly in back of the Rusiska's property and not far from the railroad tracks where it then flowed back under the tracks and became part of Touby's Run. There was a fairly large tree that had fallen on the north bank and projected directly out over the pool. We used to have fun climbing out on that tree and daring ourselves to not fall! Somehow, there were small fish in the pool. Whether or not George "seeded" the pool with them or whether they were there through an act of God, we were fishing for them that sunny afternoon! I don't remember there being any fish in the pool as I grew older, so I think George might have been the culprit! I believe that Kenny and I each caught a fish that we were required to place back in the pond. It was a wonderful day!!

One story about the fireplace, that I actually witnessed, evolved around my fearless friend, Danny Maglott (remember him from the storm drain story?). Dan was never one to avoid taking chances in the name of having fun, so he decided, after checking out the dimensions, that he could enter the chimney top of the brick fireplace opening and exit the fireplace at the bottom. Well, we didn't believe that he could do it, as the opening of the chimney was only about 12" x 18" and there was a 90-degree bend at the grill! Needless to say, after numerous "I dare you to's" were issued, he climbed to the top of the chimney, put his feet down through the opening, and proceeded to "wriggle" his way down. Much to our surprise, he was doing fairly well...until he hit the 90-degree bend at the grill! Keep in mind that we, as humans, had our knees designed by God, to have a lot of flexibility bending backward, but none bending forward. There were some very tense and agonizing moments as poor Danny, stuck as he was, lost all his bravado and began to whimper (scream?), "I can't get out"! Alas, as observers, we were torn between having to tell our parents about the current situation, or just keep hoping that good old Danny would pull this scheme off too! Luckily, (or by the hand of the good Lord), Danny somehow got unstuck (a miracle?) and "wriggled" his way out of the grill opening unscathed, except for some fairly nasty scratches on his back! Way to go, Danny!!

Chapter Thirteen
Winter Time, Fun Time

03/13/09

Winter on Harvard Avenue was always full of fun things to do, most of them outdoor activities. As kids, my sisters, Susan and Jeanne, and I would ask our Mom, almost daily, if it was supposed to snow. If she read that the Mansfield News Journal weather report said that there was a "chance of snow", we would become excited at the possibility. Usually, if the snow didn't appear or appeared as "flurries" we would be disappointed, but always remained hopeful for the big snowfall! When we did get the big snowfall, our most fun activity was getting dressed in our snowsuits with our hats, gloves, and boots and heading out to go sled riding. Harvard Avenue was the perfect venue for sled riding!! It had a long, fast decline beginning up the street by the Miller's house and if the conditions were just right, one could slide down the hill to and past the Schroeders! The snow would bring out almost every kid on the street and a riot of sleds and snowsuits would be seen for the better part of the day! Snowball fights were not uncommon along the route and "crack the whip", which was when four or five sleds would be hooked together by the boots inserted into the front of the next sled in line. The lead sled would then turn sharply from side to side on the way down the hill and try to dislodge the remainder of the sleds in the line. Laughter, combined with the occasional crying bout, could be heard throughout the day. Even though there was the occasional accident or two, we mostly just shrugged off the pain and kept right on sledding. Races between two or three sleds were also a lot of fun. My sisters and I had a sled called the "Lightning Guider" which almost always proved to be the fastest sled on the street.

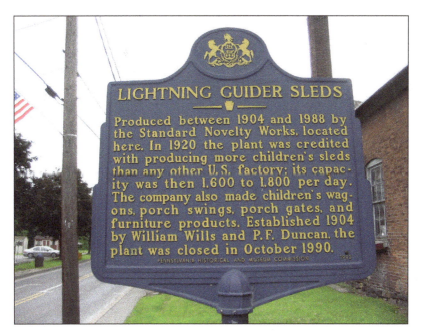

Lightning Guider manufacturer

Although it wasn't the newest or the biggest sled, something about it allowed it to be quick. I remember Susan and I would argue over which one of us would get to use the Lightning Guider and which of us would have to use the newer, bigger, but considerably slower Flexible Flyer sled that our Grandma Emma had bought us one year. I don't remember how we obtained the Lightning Guider. The winner of the argument was usually the one who could keep his younger sister from complaining to Mom... Back when it would snow, the city would send around a fleet of dump trucks loaded with coal ash from the power plants that used to burn coal to make electricity. They didn't use road salt at that time. If we were enjoying a particularly great day of sledding, occasionally a city truck would be spotted at the bottom of the hill on Tudor Street, ready to make its run-up to Harvard Avenue. Back then, because we lived at the western edge of the city limits and on a dead-end street, we didn't get the coal ash treatment as often as some of the busier neighborhoods might.

When a city truck was spotted, we would all run down the hill screaming and waving our arms to stop the driver from ruining our fun. The nice thing was, they would sometimes have pity on us fun-loving kids and would turn around and drive away! When we weren't successful, or the sun had melted the snow on our street, we had another great alternative place to sled. This run was located behind the houses on the east side of Harvard Avenue. It began in the backyard of a house on Grasmere Avenue on a small, flat concrete patio, of someone who understood the joy of kids sled riding! They never complained that we used their patio as our launching pad and I don't think that they had any kids that were in our group. They were just nice people! The run left their concrete patio and went down their backyard through the Kuhn's and Maglott's backyards through the Popp's and, if it was a particularly good ride, ended at the northern side of the

Theaker's house across the street from the McLaughlin's (which was on the north side of Harvard Avenue). We would often build ramps along the run in the Maglott's backyard and would occasionally jump off of them if we had the courage, or slide around them if we didn't. We also, from time to time, tried to develop sliding hills in the woods behind our house, but they were never successful. Occasionally, we would be driven to Middle Park where there was a gigantic hill running down to a creek that meandered from South Park to Middle Park and through to North Lake Park. It was a very fast but short ride to the bottom and if one wasn't careful, they could end up in the shallow creek bed after an unceremonious fall of three feet!

Me, my sisters and our friends would also make "snow angels" in our front yard on the newly fallen snow. Every winter, my Mom would decorate the inside of our house with whatever decorations were available. One of my fondest memories of this time was of her placing fiberglass "snow" on our mantle top on which she would place wax candles that had the appearance of angels singing Christmas carols. She would also place small round ornaments of gold, blue, and red in the snow along with small green Christmas trees were made of material that looked like a bristle brush. Early on, when we were old enough, we were allowed to put Glasswax stencils on the panes of the front picture window. Glasswax was a product that, for the rest of the year, was used for cleaning glass windows, but at Christmas, they marketed stencils of various Christmas items such as trees, bells, reindeer, etc. After dabbing it on the windows through the stencils, it would dry to a pink powdery finish and I remember it had a slightly sweet fragrance all its own.

At Christmas, as a boy of nine or ten years old and before becoming an altar boy at St. Peters, I became a "flambeau" which is French for, "flame boy". We would be invited to participate in midnight mass on Christmas Eve. There were probably thirty or forty of us boys. We would be dressed in black cassocks and white surplices and we would march to the front of the church from the rear vestibule with lighted candles in our hands. The overhead lights were dimmed for this procession, and Mom always loved this part of the mass. I'm sure she was proud of me for being a flambeau! However, you could dress a nine-year-old up, but you couldn't rein him in for the two-hour service without some consequences. One year, me and my best friend at St. Peters, Billy Jordan, (we used to have a lot of fun together), had marched to the front of the church and were seated in pews, which used to line either side of the Nave. Well, we began to giggle about something, no doubt hilarious to a nine year old, and Billy dipped his head to hide his laughter and his hair (crew cuts were fashionable then) touched the flame of the lighted candle with predictable results! He hurriedly brushed his hair with his hand as tiny sparks flew. An odor of burnt hair permeated the Nave for a few seconds, and Billy and I tried our hardest to keep a straight face for the remainder of the service! When I was in the fourth or fifth grade, I was recruited by Sister Giovani to become a member of the boy's choir. Sister Giovani was probably eighteen or nineteen years old, just out of Joliet, Illinois (the home base of the Franciscan Sisters), stood about five feet tall, and was as diminutive as could be. Oh, and she was so pretty! I, along with a few of my choirmates, had quite the crush on her! She would lead choir practices in the former school library on the eighth floor of the old grade school building. There we would learn Catholic hymns by rote and she would drill us constantly until we became an excellent choir! I was designated as a high soprano (my voice hadn't begun to change) which sang the very high parts of certain hymns. At Christmas, we would join the men's choir to sing at midnight mass. One year, our reputation had grown so that WMAN, the local radio station, would broadcast the midnight mass live! My Mom was so proud and excited! She told me after the mass that we sounded beautiful and that she heard me singing the high parts of Adestes Fidelis and Silent Night in Latin!! Maybe she could or maybe couldn't, but it didn't really matter, I believed her anyway.

Christmas day was made all the more wonderful as we would go up to Grandma Emma's house each season where we would get to mingle with our aunts, uncles, and cousins, most of whom we only saw once or twice a year. When we were very young, Moms' older brother, my uncle Raymond, lived in Georgetown, Ohio on the Ohio River (the family later moved to Bellefontaine, Ohio). He and his wife Aunt Eve, had three children: Tommy, who was four years older than me, and the twins Peggy and Greggy, who were my sister Susans' age. Uncle Raymond's kids were very nice, but they were like fish out of water whenever they came to the "big city" to visit and I think they disapproved of us Mansfield cousins and had a hard time trying to relate to us "city slickers". Uncle Raymond was an Ohio State Highway Patrolman and he always seemed stern to me, although I'm sure he wasn't really as he was usually involved in some sort of uproarious laughter with Grandma Emma and his siblings! Mom's youngest brother, Uncle Jimmie, lived in Indianapolis, Indiana with his wife, Aunt Irene, and his four children: Linda, who was Susan's age, Karin, who was a little younger than Jeanne, and the twins, Mike and Bruce. Uncle Jimmies' kids were always pretty quiet and I think they were often overwhelmed by us Adamescu Kids who were usually rambunctious and a little louder. Uncle Jimmie had a Ph.D. in microbiology from the Ohio State University in Columbus, Ohio, and worked his entire career with the Eli Lilly Company, the giant pharmaceutical firm. Mom was very proud of all her brothers, but I think Jimmie was somehow special in her eyes because of his accomplishments. Mom's oldest brother, Uncle Paul, lived out on the northside of town on Eby Road, not far from where Grandma Emma and her siblings grew up on their Grandfather Theodore Schettler's farm (this farm was later sold to the Ohio State Reformatory to be used as part of their "honor farm" where good inmates could work in a more peaceful situation).

The family then moved to South Main Street in Mansfield. The farm was located on the old Sandusky Road, now known as North Main Street. Uncle Paul and his wife, Aunt Mary, were not able to have children of their own and so adopted a son, Lloyd, and a daughter, Kristen. We often saw Lloyd and Kristen as they were similar in age to my brothers and sisters and visited Grandma Emma frequently at her house on Home Avenue. Lloyd was a farm boy at heart while Kristen was a shy girl who always had a sweet smile on her face. Their parent's home was part of their Grandma Mahon's (Mary's mother) family farm, which was near the old Schettler farm.

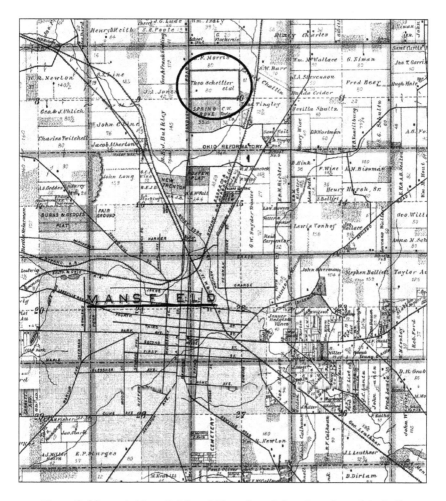

Map of old north Mansfield and Theodore Schettlers farm (circled)

The house was protected by a large orange cat named "Jackson" who was always around and who lived to a ripe old age of eighteen. On the left side as we entered the driveway was the "chowhouse," a nice screened-in affair, with a concrete floor and a huge stone fireplace on one end. My Dad helped Uncle Paul build the chowhouse. During these cookouts, I would get to meet some of my Moms cousins, aunts, and uncles whom I never saw the rest of the time. The first cookout I can remember must have been between the time that Grandma Emma's husband Jimmie Sellers passed away and when she married Oscar Spell. I would guess it was between 1953 and 1955. Aunt Clara (Grandma Emma's sister) and her son Harold Leopold (Mom's cousin), arrived in a 1929 LaSalle auto that Harold owned. My memory was that Harold was very quiet and shy and that Aunt Clara was somewhat domineering. Aunt Freida (Grandma Emma's sister) and Uncle Bill would come down from Dearborn, Michigan. Bill always bought a new car every three years and he had a gregarious, if not slightly creepy personality. Aunt Frieda reminded me of Grandma Emma, both in personality and in looks, although Aunt Frieda was slightly smaller than Grandma Emma. I remember Uncle Theodore (Grandma Emma's brother) as a very tall, quiet man, but I recall little else about him. Aunt Nettie was there, as she traded time between Grandma Emma in Mansfield and Aunt Frieda in Dearborn, Michigan. Uncle Herbert (Grandma Emma's brother) was a municipal judge in Mansfield but I don't remember him being at the country cookouts. As a large part of our family's "claim to fame", he married Lauren Bacall and Humphrey Bogart at Malabar farm in Lucas in the mid-forties.

13) My great uncle Herbert with Bacall and Bogart.

14) Bromfield, Bogart and his mother, Bacall with her mother and father, my Great uncle Herbert

It seems that Uncle Herbert was a good friend of Louis Bromfield, the Pulitzer Award-winning author, who hailed from West Third Street in Mansfield, and who owned Malabar Farm. Aunt Florence (Grandma Emma's sister) was there, but I recall nothing about her. The most intense memory I have of visiting Uncle Paul and Aunt Mary was the wonderful smell of freshly brewed coffee wafting from their kitchen, which I remember as being rather narrow and leading to the back door of their house. The Schettler country cookouts were part of a long-ago past in this country, where families gathered and had houses purposely adorned with covered front porches, closely aligned on a street in a neighborhood, where neighbors could stop, almost any time of the day or evening and converse. Sadly those days are gone forever.

Chapter Fourteen
The Old Baltimore & Ohio Railroad Tracks

04/02/09

As a small child I can recall lying in bed early in the morning listening to the sound of the old steam locomotives as they rounded the bend under the Park Avenue West overpass coming from the north by North Lake Park and Sandusky, Ohio. The grade increased slightly beginning around Trimble Road and the old engines would struggle against the slight incline with a "chuf...chuf...chuf...chuf...chuuuuuffffff..." as the wheels would spin on the steel tracks trying to gain traction against the heavy load it was carrying down to Butler, Ohio. I still fondly recall those old trains, which around the time I was five or six, were being replaced by newer, more efficient, and powerful diesel locomotives. The smell of the coal burning in the bellies of the huge engines would hang in the air for some time, especially on a damp fall day. That smell was one of a kind, and I haven't smelled anything like it for a long time now, just as I haven't enjoyed the smell of burning leaves hanging in the heavy air, which is how my Dad would get rid of them back then. My Dad would burn them in a trash barrel in the backyard or in the street next to the concrete curbs. One year, the leaves burned a little too long and the asphalt melted in front of our driveway! Living next to the woods, all the fallen leaves were the one thing that was in great supply each fall. We kids would rake them into outlines of rooms in a house and we would pretend that we were living in some great mansion as we sat on the ground in one room or another. There was nothing quite as colorful or pretty as the midday sun shining on the various colors of the leaves as they lay spread around on the ground. The smell of the air on a crisp, sunny, fall day was wonderful!

We boys used to wait for a train to be passing and we would place pennies or nickels on the track so the train would run them over. We were amazed at how the weight of the train would flatten the coins out and all but obliterate the portraits of Lincoln and Jefferson on them! Just west of the tracks lay Touby's Run, a stream that begins its life as a branch of the Black Fork River just west of Newman Street at the terminus of Spring Street in the eastern flats. It runs west, passing under Route 13/Main Street just east of Oak Hill Cottage, continues it's run just north of North Lake Park and passes behind our house. Each spring, as the snow would melt, the stream would become more of a river and we kids would play on the banks next to the water, or occasionally, in the water. A portion of the base of Touby's Run behind our house was composed of very fine grayish clay, which was great for making pretend plates and cups! We would place large boulders in the water creating cascades of little waterfalls. We would fashion little sailboats out of leaves and twigs and set them off sailing towards who knows where. Great, very wet, fun was had by all until the coldness of the water began to freeze our gloveless hands and we would embark upon travels homeward to our cozy houses.

I recall that, in 1957 or 1958, a crew was dispatched to rebuild and recondition the railroad track bed behind our house. The crew worked at removing old rail and ties and replacing them with new ones and then adding a new base under them using the cinder from spent burned coal. We had a wonderful time that summer talking to the track crew and watching them from the hill next to the tracks as they went about their work. One of the best results of watching them came when one of the crew asked us if we would like to see the inside of a caboose they were using as an onsite office! It was very cool and had a plain wooden bench on one wall and a small coal-fired heater on the other side. An old kerosene lantern hung near the rear door of the caboose. The caboose smelled faintly of the coal smoke that the engines made as they traveled their route. This was during the time that cabooses were still necessary for the safe movement of trains on their journeys. Alas, as we all know, cabooses were gone from the scene by the early 1970s as technology took over for the signalman stationed at the rear of the train.

Whenever we would play on or near the tracks, we were always on the lookout for treasures hidden alongside. We would often find glass insulators from the telegraph poles that lined the trackside or heavy cast metal connectors shaped like an elongated "J" that would hold the rails to the metal tie plates below. Occasionally, the weight of the trains passing over the tracks would loosen the large metal spikes used to attach the rails to the ties and we would go home with another souvenir! Another item we would occasionally see along the tracks were

.22 caliber shell casings. Remember, this was once open farmland and shooting guns was legal. As the area surrounding the tracks developed, the city limits were moved westward to Home Road. When we first moved onto Harvard Avenue, the city limits were the railroad tracks behind our house. Not long after, shooting guns in the woods was outlawed.

The old Park Avenue West bridge that crossed over the B&O tracks was built in 1926, as was stated on an old bronze capital that was emblazoned in the NE corner of the bridge.

Map of early Park Avenue West and the rest stop for early travelers

Before that, Park Avenue West dipped down to cross the tracks at an old-style railroad crossing with flashing warning lights. Park Avenue West was a two-lane brick road when we first moved onto Harvard Avenue, as was Grasmere Avenue, until sometime in the early 1960s when it was paved over in concrete.

The Old Baltimore & Ohio Railroad Tracks

There were old houses on either side of Park Avenue West, some of which still existed when I was young. Just to the west, over the bridge, and to the north, stood an old brick house set back from the road with a stone driveway leading up to it and surrounded by very large, tall evergreen trees. As a child, I would wonder who lived in this place, which reminded me of a castle in the forest! Across from the house sat an old Department of Highways rest area, complete with an old-fashioned latrine for use by travelers on their way back from a trip to Crestline or perhaps from Marion, Ohio. It was covered with a roof and sides that were open at the top and had a squeaky door, closed by a long diagonal spring. Whenever we would ride our bikes across the bridge to the new shopping center, we would stop on the way back at the rest area, mostly for grins and giggles. The rest area smelled to high heaven most of the time until the "honey dippers" would come and clean out the latrine and as kids, we thought that this smell was somehow hilarious! There was also an old drinking fountain connected to an old-fashioned well pump that we would play with, the sole purpose of which turned out to be getting each other soaked with the well water, which always smelled of rotten eggs!

Chapter Fifteen
Joseph and Mary Adamescu Come to America

05/02/09

My Grandfather Adamescu came to America from Hitias, Romania which is about 20 miles west of Timisoara, for the first time in 1912. He stayed with his older brother Paul in the "syndicate" which was north of Fifth Street and ran to the flats. This is where many immigrants of that period settled in Mansfield to establish themselves before moving on to seek their livelihoods. Great Uncle Paul owned a house in a row of very old houses on Lily Street in the north end in the flats, very near the Ohio Brass Company. This portion of Lily Street was abandoned in the early 60's and was replaced by the very large silos on North Main Street which have "Welcome to Mansfield" painted on their sides. This was how most Eastern European immigrants came to live in Mansfield. Great Uncle Paul was Grandpa's "sponsor" and he helped Grandpa get a job as a laborer here in town. Grandpa Joe worked and saved his money and then went back to Romania and brought back his wife, (Grandma) Mary, in 1917 on the steamship, the USS Pennsylvania. They had a daughter, Anna, who was born in Romania and was probably in her early teens at this time. She decided to stay in Romania, probably because of a love interest of some sort. We never did learn how this decision affected Grandpa and Grandma Adamescu, but I'm sure it was not a pleasant separation. I still have many relatives in Romania near Hitias, many of which are no doubt the progeny of our aunt Anna. Grandpa was a game warden on a preserve in the Hitias area and thus had a real "knack" for gardening and hunting. After they had settled on Lily Street, my Uncle Paul was born, in 1918, followed by Dad, Joe, in 1921 and my Uncle John, in 1925. I believe that sometime after my Dad's birth, they moved to 268 South Adams Street, on the corner of Dale Avenue, into a house that was already almost a century old. This house stayed in our family's possession until my Dad died in 1992. Before this, it was occupied by a very old lady and somewhere in our archives, exists a picture of her in the distant past standing in front of the house wearing a long black coat in the snow.

Picture of the woman who sold the South Adams Street house to my Grandparents

We later came to find out that Grandpa Adamescu had two brothers, Paul (mentioned above) and John, who his sons would be named after. I was then named after his son, my Uncle John. My Grandpa Adamescu was good to his sons. He bought Uncle Paul a violin with which he took lessons and because of his skill, took classes at the University of Cincinnati School of Music. He even bought my Dad an airplane! He purchased it from someone in Columbus, Ohio. It was a 1924 Driggs "Skylark" and my Dad was only 18 years old!

Dad and his Driggs Skylark

He also provided my Uncle John with dance classes. The neighborhood on South Adams Street became a large mixture of ethnicities. The Marinelli boys, including their son Frank, became good friends with Dad and his brothers. The small lawns in the neighborhood were always neatly manicured with flowers, fruit trees, grapevines, and various religious statues everywhere! My Grandpa Adamescu was an industrious sort and ended up with a job at the Mansfield Tire and Rubber Company, from where he retired after 48 years. His last job was as an elevator operator, and the Mansfield Tire Magazine, which he used to receive every month at his house, has a picture of him operating the elevator! I still have the magazine that shows him in action! I remember when as a small boy of four or five, I would go with my Dad in our 1947 Pontiac Streamliner to pick up Grandpa Adamescu at the Tire late at night, as Grandpa Adamescu was then working the 3:00-11:00 pm shift. He would be waiting for us at the Wayne Street guard shack and would have his black metal lunchbox with him as he climbed into the bench seat next to Dad. I would be in the back seat, usually very sleepy, as we pulled up. I remember the old Pontiac had a heater under the front seat that would warm the rear of the car very nicely on cold winter days. I would huddle on the rear floor as we drove home to South Adams Street. I would nod off to the sound of them conversing in Romanian and from the street lights intermittently glowing on the floor of the car as we passed each one in turn. Grandma Mary worked in a cigar factory in downtown Mansfield. Grandpa Adamescu managed to purchase an additional lot behind his house where he built a garage to store my Dad's plane and where, after many years, he would put in a beautiful garden including fruit trees. At the west end of the property stood a row of currant bushes, which were used by neighbors to make jelly. All in all, Grandpa Adamescu had one of the largest lots on the street! The small house on South Adams Street already had a kitchen which was added on in the late 1800s, but my Grandpa Adamescu added a small bathroom off the kitchen and a small entryway off the back of the house after they moved into the house in the early 1920s. I have met some people who used to live in the area back then as children and one of them, an older lady who lived on Dale Avenue, told me of how Grandpa Adamescu would hunt in the fall and then butcher in the backyard, hanging the meat on curing racks for all to see! It was quite the annual event! She also mentioned that he made some of the best smoked sausages for miles around! I remember my Dad once told me that there would be sausage curing in the upstairs of the house and that he and his brothers would go up and snap off a piece to eat when they got hungry! On the south side of the yard, Grandpa Adamescu had arranged white painted bricks into a circular, vertical "soldier pattern" and had beautiful flowers planted in the center. I remember this was still in place when I was very young and I remember thinking how neat it looked.

In front of the house, bordering South Adams Street was a low hedge of some sort of prickly bushes that I would be recruited to trim after Grandpa Adamescu passed away. Grandma Adamescu was a wonderful woman, but she could be very particular. I remember trying my hardest to please her with my trimming efforts while at the same time, trying my hardest to keep from being stuck by the darn bushes. At the very northeast corner of the lot and out past the sidewalk of Dale and South Adams Streets, was a very large tree (probably 70+ years old), planted no doubt way before cars roamed the area...I mean, a person couldn't see the oncoming street to make the turn in a car! It was eventually taken down by the city (around 1955), but it was a remnant of a time in Mansfield from long ago. I remember feeling sad when, as a child, I saw the stump of the tree, level with the ground, after it had been cut down. Grandma Adamescu used to hold court from her front porch, saying "hello" to all the passers-by, sitting comfortably in a canvas and wood chair, next door to the front room of the house. Mrs. McCune lived across Dale Avenue from Grandma Adamescu, and I remember her as being very nice to us. Mrs. Kingston, a Southern lady with a southern drawl and a sweet disposition, lived across the street from South Adams Street from Grandma Adamescu. She lived in Grandma Emma's brother, Great Uncle Eds, old house. She became fast and close friends with Grandma Adamescu after Grandpa Adamescu passed away in July 1960.

Chapter Sixteen
Grandma Adamescu and Me

06/01/09

Grandma Adamescu was a wonderful, sweet woman with a huge heart, who never lost her humble beginnings. Being around her taught us that there was another world out there which had never caught up with the hustle, bustle, and materialism of modern-day America. Whenever we would visit her, she would be sitting alone in her rocking chair in the living room of her house, or maybe cooking chicken soup or sarma (sarma was eastern European and was a mixture of ground meat mixed with cabbage sauerkraut) on her gas stove in the kitchen. The greatest thing about staying at Grandma Adamescu's overnight was that in the morning she would make hot tea and serve it to me in a huge cup (remember, this was when I was five or six years old)! Grandma Adamescu had a liking for sugar, and she would put many spoonfuls and copious amounts of milk in the mixture. Then she would toast some delicious Stimmler Bakery bread and put big pats of real creamery butter on the slices! I was in heaven as we sat at her kitchen table covered in a bright, floral patterned oilcloth enjoying our breakfast! I remember the old

Servel, gas-powered refrigerator, that kept the milk and butter ice cold! When we were very young, she would still, once a year, bake the most delicious and scrumptious poppy seed and cheese strudel rolls that I have ever had! My Mom tried to get her to give her the recipe for these delicacies, but Grandma Adamescu could only tell Mom that she used a "lilly"* bit of this and a "lilly"* bit of that in her recipes, so the tradition of having these scrumptious loaves, once a year, faded as Grandma Adamescu grew older and more infirm. She especially liked the weekly "Life Is Worth Living" television show on the old Dumont network hosted by his excellency, Bishop Fulton J. Sheen. She liked to watch "Queen For a Day" with Jack Bailey on NBC which Susan and I would often watch with her after school. Susan and I would be picked up by our Uncle Paul after his job was done at Westinghouse during the week. We would walk down First Street from St. Peters' School to a little viaduct that ran under the road with our cousins Nick, Joe, Bill, and Thais and wait there for him to pick us up. Uncle Paul would drop us off at Grandma Adamescus' house to wait for Dad to take us home after Dad's day's with work were done. Uncle Paul then drove his kids to their house on Agate Avenue, which ran north off of South Diamond Street a few miles further on. One of Grandma Adamescus' favorite television shows was the old wrestling matches that she would watch religiously every single week.

    She was horrified by the staged choreography where the wrestlers would hit each other and I think she might have believed that they were truly hurting each other. She had a morbid curiosity about the wrestlers though and would often interject a disparaging "clucking" noise whenever a more egregious body slam would occur. Some of her favorite wrestlers back then were

Gorgeous George, Killer Kowalski, Bruno Sammartino, and BoBo Brazil, whose trademark "CoCoButt" would really set her off!! Grandma Adamescu was a religious soul and always told us "Jesus, he loves for you"*. I know that in my case at least, she helped me to get through some tough times when I was younger by convincing me that this was true. Whenever my Dad would get especially "tough" with us around her, she would always admonish him to stop by imploring "lassa, Joe, lassa". I'm not sure what this meant, but I always thought it meant "easy, Joe, easy". Whenever we would leave her house Dad would say, "shivud" to her, which we interpreted to mean 'goodbye".

After Grandpa Adamescu passed away in 1960, I was often recruited to go up to Grandma Adamescu's house and help her with chores that she could no longer manage. I was eleven years old at the time and looking back, this was a way that I was taught respect and responsibility by my Dad. I often would be required to stay overnight and work the entire next day on her list of things to do. I would wash all of her windows on the outside (she still cleaned them on the inside), I would have to trim and rake the aforementioned pricker bushes in front of her yard, I would cut her grass, clean out her flower beds, and would take side trips to the little store a small block away, that was at the top of Dale Avenue on South Diamond Street. Whenever I went to the store, known as "Georges" it was to buy her soda pop, a luxury that I think was forbidden when Grandpa Adamescu was still living. Her request was always for "three or-orange and three roots beer". She would allow me to spend 25 cents on an ice cream cone and I always bought myself a fudge ripple cone. Occasionally, she would have me bring her a cone too and, in the summer, it became a race to get back to her house before the cone began to melt! During the year, whenever we would visit her with Dad, she would always have a bag of penny candy in her Hoosier Hutch in the kitchen that she would share with us as we left on our way home. When I slept over, my bed would be the old green couch in her living room. We would listen to WMAN on the radio with the lights out, and only the yellowish-orange glow of the radio dial, to see by until around 9:00 PM, and then we would go to bed. She slept upstairs in the big old featherbed with a huge, feather-stuffed pillow. I remember lying on the couch before falling asleep listening to the sound of the occasional car driving by, through the open front screen door, or the city bus that would stop directly across the street before moving on to downtown. The street light cast shadows across the living room walls that I would study before nodding off. I truly believe that, when Grandma Adamescu died in 1968, God must have taken her straight to heaven!

*(me trying, very poorly, to put Grandma Marys' Romanian accent into English)

Chapter Seventeen
Grandpa Adamescu and Me

07/20/09

As a child, my Grandpa Adamescu always seemed like a very stern man to me. As a matter of fact, even though I loved him, I was always tentatively afraid of him. However, he was an excellent nurseryman and gardener and when we had first moved out onto Harvard Avenue in 1949, he was in heaven with the large lot behind our house.

He took approximately 60% of the backyard and turned it into a beautiful nursery garden with a myriad of vegetables and many types of fruit trees! I remember sweet yellow corn, green peppers, tomatoes, red and white radishes, beets, cucumbers, different varieties of squash, string beans, peas, carrots, and lettuce. There were two pear trees, two peach trees, an apple tree to which he had grafted two varieties of apples, two purple plum trees, and a black cherry tree, and at the back of the lot, he had planted both red and black raspberry bushes! During the summer months beginning when I was four or five, as the string beans had matured, he would "recruit" me to help him snap off and dispose of the stringy ends and then break the beans in half.

Memories of a Baby Boomer from Mansfield

Grandpa Adamescu and me in our new backyard in 1950

For some reason, we always did this in our living room with a bushel basket full of beans, an old newspaper on the floor, and a paper grocery sack in which to place the broken beans. I remember him spraying the fruit trees in the spring and summer with a long, hand-pump-operated sprayer that had a hose that was placed into a large bucket full of some sort of bug-repellent chemical. He always wore a straw hat with a green visor built into the front brim and he would wrap a bandana around his mouth and nose while he was spraying the trees. I was allowed to watch him, but he always made sure that I stayed a safe distance from him and had the wind (if there was any) at my back. My Mom and Grandma Emma used to can and "put up" in Mason jars, peaches, beans, corn, and tomato juice. I believe that they also occasionally made a few jars of bread and butter pickles, from the cucumbers, and jars of vegetable soup! We kept these canned goods in the "fruit cellar" in our basement, which was located under the basement stairs. I remember Mom and Grandma Emma boiling (sterilizing) the Mason jars on the stove in large pots and placing paraffin wax on top of the jars before sealing them with the lids. The lids were a way to tell if the food was sealed correctly as they would "pop" if the seal was broken. There was a large tulip tree in the front corner of the garden next to the Rusiskas that would produce beautiful, large, purple, and white flowers each year.

Mom had a pink dogwood tree planted at the back of the garage and a white dogwood tree at the very back of our lot that Grandpa Adamescu wanted to cut down, but Mom put her foot down and it remained in place...It is still alive today, almost seventy-three years later! Behind the white dogwood tree stood an old chestnut tree that used to drop chestnuts every year in the late summer. They were green and had a "suede" like finish to them that, when scratched, gave off a wonderful aroma! Grandpa Adamescu became ill around 1955 or 1956 with congestive heart failure and progressively got sicker until he could no longer tend to his beloved garden. My Dad, not being a gardener, left the fruit trees and garden go and after Grandpa Adamescu died in July of 1960, the garden and trees fell into neglect and eventually they all died. Mom told me that Grandpa Adamescu urged her to admonish Dad to take care of the garden and fruit trees, which she did, but to no avail. God bless my Grandpa Adamescu!

Chapter Eighteen
Summer Play

06/01/15

In the summer when we were young, one of the most fun things to do was to go out and play when there was heavy rain. Mom wouldn't let us go if lightning was in the air, but if it wasn't, we would join several other neighborhood kids in the street to build dams from rocks in the concrete gutter next to the curb. We would watch leaf boats that we would make as they floated away down the street in the streams of water. Often, towards the end of a storm, the sun would come out and there would appear a beautiful rainbow over the Maglott and Kuhn houses to the southeast. When it was very hot, and I remember it being very hot at times in the summer, we would ask Mom to allow us to run through the sprinkler in the front yard. Sometimes, she would say no because it used too much water, but often she would hook it up and we would take turns running and jumping over the whirling sprinkler blades or slowly placing our hands over the whirling nozzles to stop it from spinning. We also used to play red rover, hide and seek, spud, and other games that would occupy us for hours! Danny Maglott and I used to play a game we called "Andy, Andy, over" by tossing a rubber ball back and forth over his garage to the person on the other side. The goal was to catch the ball without it hitting the ground. Sounds pretty simple, but it was always hard to tell just where the ball might appear from the other side, so it was a challenge and we would play this game often. We boys also used to play a game called "mumbly peg" which required one of us to own a pocket knife. In this game, two of us would stand about three feet apart, facing each other. The one who had the knife to begin the game would throw the knife at the feet of the other player and if the knife stuck in the ground, the attacked player had to extend his stance to that point. The game would continue until one player lost his balance or could no longer stretch to meet the knife point in the ground. Sometimes, this game would deteriorate to each person trying to get as close as possible to the extended foot of his opponent, with predictable consequences. We also would play "50 cents" in the street with a ball, a bat, and a glove. In turn, we would each be in the "outfield" as another friend would hit the ball to us. I remember that if we successfully caught a grounder it would be worth 25 cents, a line drive was worth 50 cents, and a fly ball would bring $1.00. The goal was to accumulate more money than your opponents did and we usually played this game in the street in front of Mr. Clines' house.

Chapter Nineteen

My Father's Call to 5:00 AM Sunday Mass

06/02/15

When we were very young, most of us Adamescu boys had a Sunday ritual that was imposed upon us by our Dad. We were required to attend 5:00 am mass with him each week. This meant that we would be awakened around 4:15 am, told to get dressed and brush our teeth and be ready to leave our house for St. Peter's church around 4:30 am. God help us if we weren't ready on time! Our Dad directed us out of fear of what could happen to us if we didn't follow orders and, as young boys, we learned our lessons well. We would arrive twenty minutes before mass began and we would always sit in the last pew at the back of the church on St. Joseph's side right by the large front doors of the church. This was an uncomfortable situation in the winter as, each time the large doors were opened, cold air would rush in and chill us to the bone. One of Dad's pet peeves, among many others as it turned out, was a fidget-prone kid. This made an uncomfortable time as Dad would shoot us one of his (to us) terrifying glares if we moved. Additionally, because I had undiagnosed allergies, I tended to sniff at a pretty regular rate and this was not acceptable to him at all. Going to church with Dad became a stressful chore after a while. I was hugely relieved when my brother Tim was old enough to inherit my spot next to Dad at mass.

However, all was not negative about Sunday mornings with Dad. Occasionally, we would stop at a bakery on South Main Street run by a very nice, old-world German man, who made the most delightful pastries and cookies. The bakery was located just north of the Rt. 42 split on the east side of Main Street. We would buy cream horns, strudels, and my favorite, German butter cookies! These trapezoidal-shaped cookies with a dusting of coarse sugar and cinnamon were delicious! The old baker would place the pastries in a white box and tie it off with white string that hung down from the ceiling. When we arrived home it was now daylight and my Mom was up and had coffee brewing and breakfast cooking. I was probably 8 or 9 when I was finally allowed to have a little coffee with my butter cookies and dunking them in the coffee only enhanced their wonderful taste to me! A few years before, we had a pet dog named "Sparky".

Sparky lying by the side of our new house

I was very young, but I remember him as a medium to large dog with long blondish hair. One Saturday evening, when I was 4 or 5, Sparky didn't return home from his daily jaunt. We didn't know where he was and I remember my Mom being concerned. The next morning, on our way to Sunday mass, Dad and I spotted him lying on his left side on the north side of Park Avenue West right at Middle Park. He had been hit by a car and was dead. Dad told me that he was gone and that we would pick him up on our way back from church. After we brought him home, Mom and Dad had him buried at the Angel Refuge on Park Avenue West in Ontario, Ohio. This place was run by the Workman sisters, whom

I remember as being rather large, not well-groomed women, but very nice and very sympathetic to Sparky and us. Sparky was buried in the Angel Refuge cemetery and had a touchstone placed on his grave by my parents. Whenever we would travel out of Ontario, on our way home, we could see the cemetery from the road to remind us of Sparky.

Chapter Twenty
A New Shopping Center, Kindergarten, John Gets Lost

06/03/2015

When Dad and Mom moved onto Harvard Avenue in 1950, our development was at the extreme west end of the Mansfield city limits. That all began to change in 1954. Land was purchased at the south side of Park Avenue West across the bridge to construct one of the first "shopping centers" in our area. West Park Shopping Center began construction in the fall of 1955. I remember hearing, through the trees in the woods, the bulldozers and other earthmoving equipment hard at work preparing the land for the new buildings to be built. I also remember that, sometime in 1954, my Mom showed me the News Journal article with the architect's rendering of what the center would look like when finished. I believe that, with much fanfare, the grand opening happened in 1956. I remember, when I was 6 or 7, sitting on the hill at the edge of the woods by the railroad tracks and watching as a flagpole sitter, I believe his name was Bob or something, would climb to the top of the pole that must have been 90 or 100 feet tall! I was amazed as he would purposely make the pole sway from side to side as he performed his stunts. The most remarkable stunt that he did was to stand on his head while swaying back and forth! When the shopping center opened it had a First National Bank, a Kroger and Big Bear stores, a Gray Drug, a Moore's Hardware, an FW Woolworth, a State store, a Top Value Stamp store, Williams Music, and a Weidles Meats store among many others. When we were a little older, we would ride our bikes over to the center and ride up and down the sidewalk in front of the stores and often would stop at the soda fountain at Woolworth's, where my favorite refreshment was a cherry Coke for 15 cents! One other thing I distinctly remember was that there was muzak playing from the speakers in the overhang over the sidewalks. This was the first time I had experienced this type of entertainment! After the center opened, Mansfield annexed land to move the city limits out west to Home Road.

When I was 4 or 5, I went to kindergarten at Brinkerhoff School. I was very shy at this point in my life and it was hard for me to "fit in" to kindergarten. I'm sure other kids felt the same way. However, I had a very sweet, younger lady as a teacher, and she made me feel more at ease as time passed. As part of this experience, in the summer months, we were fortunate to also be able to attend Safety Town, which originated in Mansfield and was held on the green-painted, paved playground just west of Brinkerhoff School. I really enjoyed this program as we were able to learn safety rules as they applied to crossing the street, watching the street signs, and lights as well as where and how to walk. Some days, we were allowed to learn how cars moved in traffic as we rode three-wheeled tricycles around the streets, which were laid out on the pavement with white paint. A fixture at Safety Town was Officer Tom, a Mansfield policeman, who always arrived riding a white Harley Davidson motorcycle trike which reminded us of an ice cream truck! He would advise us on how to act and react to the different traffic signals and other issues of personal safety. On graduation day at kindergarten, we danced the "Hokey Pokey" and sang "Let the Ball Roll" which was a song that taught us kids to not run into the street after our toys. I remember that some of the kids took a bus to school and they wore a different colored plastic "necklace" that designated which bus they would be on for a ride home. I think Helen Rusiska would drive Kenny and me to school, as we never had to wear one of these necklaces. At five years old, I was ready for the next big step in my educational journey or should I say my age dictated that I was ready. I remember that I struggled mightily with separation anxiety during the first few weeks of first grade at St. Peter's. The first few days of school our mothers were allowed to stay, for a time, with us in the classroom. As soon as my Mom would be leaving, I would burst into tears and not want her to go home. My Mom, God bless her, was very good about getting me to face my fears and she stood lovingly firm that I had to be on my own now. After a few days of this action, I was able to stay without her. I will admit, though, that I was lonely and did miss her for some time after I was on my own. I think part of the reason that I was able to fit in was my first-grade teacher, Sister Marciana. She was a short little nun, but she was kind and able to be firm without being mean. The nuns at our school, as I stated before, were of the order of St. Francis of Jolliet, Illinois. Most of them were saints, giving their all to educate us for a pittance of monetary allowance, but they had each other and our parent's approval. It was in first grade that I met my friends at St. Peter's, almost all of whom I graduated with 12 years later!

My first grade class with our first Communion picture

As the year progressed and Mom felt that I was trustworthy, I began to take the city bus home from school each day. My Mom had arranged for me to go with my cousin Cathy, my Uncle Paul's oldest child, who was 9 years older than me and was already in high school at St. Peter's. Cathy was to escort me from school on North Mulberry Street to the square downtown, in front of Martins' Hardware where I was to pick up the Park Avenue West bus home. She would make sure I got on the right bus and then I would begin my journey homeward. I would ride the bus out Park Avenue West, over the bridge by our house, where the bus would turn around at West Park Shopping Center and begin heading back east again toward downtown. I knew that I was to pull the buzzer cord on the bus when it began to cross the bridge and the driver would stop at the corner of Park Avenue West and Grasmere Avenue and let me off. One time, it was very crowded and hectic on the square and Cathy was talking to a number of her friends. Somehow we got separated and I got on the wrong bus without Cathy's guidance. I soon realized that I didn't recognize some of the houses we were passing and I also noticed that there were very few people on what was usually a very crowded bus. I started looking around for help and I became very worried. Luckily, there was a kind older lady sitting across from me and she soon realized that I was in some sort of trouble. She asked me if I was okay and I gave her a tentative "yes". She said, "are you lost"? I told her that I thought I was on the wrong bus. She said she would help me and we got off at her stop where she then asked me for my phone number. At that point in my life, I don't think I remembered what it was, so she asked me what my name was and I told her "John Adamescu". She said, "Well let's just look that up in the telephone book". She said there were four Adamecu's listed and did I know my father's name, to which I answered, "Joe and I live on Harvard Avenue". She called my Mom and she picked me up within half an hour! Thinking back, my Mom, either because trusted me or out of sheer necessity, gave me a lot of responsibility as a child, for which I am forever thankful to her. I also know that I wouldn't trust my children in today's society to do some of the things that were possible back in a more peaceful, trusting time.

Chapter Twenty One

My Early St. Peters' Friends

06/04/2015

My world began to broaden immensely after I started school. Although I was still shy and somewhat withdrawn, I soon began to make friends and enjoy the learning experience. Most of my first-grade classmates at St. Peter's went through school with me for the next 12 years and we all graduated together. To this day, I believe that we have the closest class ever to graduate from St. Peter's! One of my first friends was Tom Vassar. By second grade, we were visiting each other for play dates and having a good time in school together. Tom lived at 96 Wolfe Avenue across from Prospect Park. His mother, Clara, had been widowed shortly after Tom was born. She was a very sweet lady and always made sure that we had fun when we were at his house. We would usually get together early on Saturday mornings and we would watch the old TV shows together. One of our favorites was "Tales of Texas Rangers". If the weather was cooperating, we would walk across the street to Prospect Park and play on the swings. Another classmate of ours, Tom Calandra, lived not far from Tom and we would play with him and his older brother, Jim.

I remember that both Tom's liked to play chess, which I hadn't even heard of before then, and a match would ensue with Tom Calandra and Tom Vassar verbally dueling each other over the game. Tom and I were close for the first couple of years, but I managed to put a kink in our relationship one day at school, and looking back, I don't blame him! We were on our usual morning lavatory break and Tom came strolling into the boy's room and said "Well, we have to go to the "s - - t" house. Digressing for a second...I think I lived a fairly sheltered life up to that point, whereas, I believe that a number of my friends were a tad bit more advanced in the ways of the world than I was. Back to the story...Well, I thought that this language was uncalled for and I proceeded to pull our second-grade teacher, Sister Willette aside, and tell her what Tom had said. I was really feeling "my oats" as the good little boy I was! However, as any arbiter might, she grabbed both of us and began to grill both of us in turn. "Tom, did you really say that?"... "No Sister, John did"... "John did you"... " No Sister, Tom did". This line of questioning went on for another two or three seconds (maybe) and then she said, "You both will have to eat soap"! We proceeded to stand at the water fountain while she retrieved a bar of Ivory hand soap. When she came back, she proceeded to carve two or three chunks of the soap and told us to eat them. I remember the horrible taste of the soap as it foamed in my mouth. She said, "Hold it in there"! After what seemed like an hour (no doubt maybe ten seconds) she told us we could spit it out in the water fountain and rinse our mouths out. I soon learned two valuable lessons: 1) discretion is the better part of valor and 2) friends don't ever rat out friends.

Another adventure that the two of us went on centered around another one of our friends, Larry Rose. Larry was tall for his age and had a huge strawberry birthmark on his face. He was also occasionally known for wearing a bolo tie to school. I don't think any of us ever commented on his birthmark, as we really liked him. The tie, well we would kid with him about that, but we soon found out that Larry lived out in the country and had horses. His parents had a little money and lived on a large lot in Lexington, Ohio where they kept the horses. One spring Saturday, a group of us kids were invited out to play at Larry's house. It was a really beautiful place and we played all morning long. When we finally stopped playing we had a great lunch of sandwiches and chips on his front lawn. Mrs. Rose was a doll! There was a creek across the road from Larry's house and we went there in the afternoon and played. Later on in the afternoon, Mrs. Rose called out to us that we would be going home in half an hour or so, and that we should come in and get cleaned up for the trip. Boy, we should have listened to her! Instead, we were having too much fun to stop. We kept playing until "the incident" happened. Tom Vassar and I were standing near the edge of the creek, no doubt tossing stones into the water, when Tom Calandra found an old, beat-up, aluminum water bucket in the dirt. For reasons unknown, perhaps to the mind of an eight-year-old caught up in the moment, he mightily heaved the bucket towards the creek. His aim was poor. The bucket came down on Tom Vassar just as he was turning in response to the command "Look out!" The bucket hit him square in the forehead opening a huge gash! Blood was everywhere! We were all either screaming or crying, a number of us running full out towards Larry's house! We were yelling "Mrs. Rose, Tom is bleeding!" She ran out with a towel, which she applied to Tom's wound. She was a tad upset, and rightly so. She told us to get our things together, get washed up, and get ready for our rides to pick us up! This time everyone obeyed her. Tom ended up in the emergency room, where he had numerous stitches applied to his head. I think we all learned a little lesson that day and we also had a blast visiting Larry's house!

Chapter Twenty-Two
Flying Kites, Catching Lightning Bugs

06/12/15

As boys, we used to wait (barely) for the March winds to begin to blow so we could fly kites up in the field. Each spring, the Connors' Westgate Pantry store would get a supply of paper kites, "Fli Hi," I think they were called. They had regular triangular kites as well as box kites, although none of us kids messed with the box kites as they were very hard to get up in the air and even harder to control. Back then, the triangular kites sold for ten cents and the box kites for fifteen cents. The kite we all wanted to buy was the one with the black Jolly Roger printed on it! It was our favorite! Unfortunately, that meant it was also in short supply, as everyone would constantly check at Connors' to see if they had arrived. We would beg our mothers for rags to use as the tails on the kites, which were a necessity, especially during very windy conditions. Sometimes, our moms couldn't supply our "stabilizers" and those kites would suffer the consequences, usually nose-diving into the ground and breaking one of their support sticks. I remember trying to scotch tape a broken stick together, but to no avail...the kite was finished. The older boys would buy 2 or 3 lengths of string to tie together so that they would be able to let their kites fly over 1,000 feet! I remember they would stand in the field, close to the Rusiska's house, and their kite would be way up in the air, and extend out to the south so that they appeared to be far over Trimble Road! Often, on a perfectly windy day, the older boys would be able to "plant" a large stick in the ground and tie off their kites to fly, unattended, while they would go home for supper! I always thought that this was the ultimate feat of magic, as, for some unknown reason, I was never able to do this myself.

During the late spring and early summer, we would go searching for grasshoppers and other assorted insects in the field. There was never a shortage of insects back then and we would capture them and put them in a mason jar with holes punched into the metal lids, to assure that the insects could breathe. We would often encounter a praying mantis, which, we were told, was protected by some law and could not be hurt, or we would suffer some unknown consequence. Also, stick bugs, that actually looked like a twig, would sometimes be found. At night, during the summer, we would go hunting for lightning bugs that we would capture and put in the jars. Since we lived right next to the woods, mosquitoes were in great abundance, and we usually had two or three bites itching somewhere on our bodies. In the hot summer, we would sweat, and this seemed to be the signal for the mosquitoes to attack! I do remember though, that after a while, the mosquitoes didn't bother us as much, as we had accepted them as part of playing outdoors. Grasshoppers were also in abundance, especially up in the field when the ground would be let to overgrow with thick grasses and weeds. Running through the field became a game of dodging the grasshoppers, as they would spring from the weeds and occasionally end up in your mouth!

When we would play catch or baseball in Rusiskas' backyard (when Helen wasn't "shooing" us away) we would lose a ball in the high grasses of the farm field. One way we used to search for the ball was, no doubt, the result of a long-held superstition handed down to young boys in the neighborhood over the years. We would get a bat and balance it on one hand (horizontally) while walking around the general vicinity of where we thought the ball was located. If the bat "tipped' to one side or the other it would indicate where the ball had landed and we would be "successful," but more often than not we would have to continue the search. I suppose that even though we were able to find the ball very rarely using this technique, it happened often enough that the legend persisted!

Chapter Twenty Three
Visits to Dr. Staker and Dr. Acomb

06/16/15

As a child, my trips to various doctors were, shall I say, exciting adventures?

They surely were for my Mom and the various doctors and nurses I would be foisted upon. I was not a model patient, and I would scream, cry and do anything I could, short of mayhem, to avoid the consequences of my visits which, at that age, were usually inoculations of some sort. This was especially true when I would go see Dr. Staker, our family General Practitioner. His office was on the northeast corner of Park Avenue West and North Mulberry Street, in a very old stone mansion that was on a fashionable Park Avenue West of the day. When I would go, however, time had turned the once beautiful facade into a dark, black edifice. In addition, there was a very steep, foreboding set of stone stairs leading up to the enormous wooden front doors! To me, it was like going to prison! Inside, the first thing I remember was the sterile smell of alcohol and other medical potions. There was a desk in the entryway for the receptionist and to the left and right were patient waiting rooms. For some

Visits to Dr. Staker and Dr. Acomb

reason, we always ended up on the left side with the windows facing Mulberry Street. From there, a swinging wooden door led to the examination room. I was fine until "Steiny" (her nickname, as her last name was Steinberger), an RN friend of my Mom's, who was Dr. Staker's assistant would call out "Johnny". This was my cue to begin whimpering, which was followed by loud crying. When Dr. Staker would appear, it was "Nellie, bar the door"! He was a nice-looking man with a completely bald head and a very kind smile. This would belie his efficiency with a syringe. I'm sure that Steiny was a wonderful, caring sort of person and a great friend to my Mother, but she would allow me no quarter and would grab me by my shoulders and pull me into a bear hug, while Dr. Staker tried to smooth my ruffled psyche. My Mom would be pleading with me to settle down, to no avail, and Steiny was commanding me to hold still or the shot would really hurt! So, I think I got my fear of the needle honestly. After the inoculation was administered, I would continue my crying jag (for the pity factor, no doubt) for a while, but I would be fine by the time we were leaving.

As I look back, I'm sure that my visits to Dr. Stakers' offices were dreaded by them as much as they were by me!

Due to our financial situation as a family, we weren't able to visit the dentist as often as my mother would have liked. Unfortunately, her teeth were neglected as a child and she lost them to false teeth around 1956. I think this gave her an extra impetus to have us visit the dentist whenever she could afford it. Our dentist was Dr. Acomb, who, as I recollect, was an older gentleman with white hair. His office was on the lower level of an office building on the southeast corner of Wood Street and Marion Avenue.

I remember it was next to a beauty parlor. When I would visit Dr. Acomb, I wasn't as afraid of him as when I would go to Dr. Stakers'. Dr. Acomb was a lot better with children, at least to me. When I would be seated in the big green dental chair, he would ask me if he could draw a face on my thumbnail with his drill. I watched in amazement as he would lightly scratch a cute smiling face on my nail! It didn't hurt at all and it put me well at ease. When I was 6 or 7, I got an abscess in one of my baby molars.

I was in pain. Mom took me to see Dr. Acomb. He explained to me that he was going to give me a little gas to put me to sleep, and then he would take out the bad tooth. I don't remember much after that except that I was very groggy when I woke up, and I could feel a hole where my molar had been and a slight metallic taste in my mouth from the blood. It didn't hurt much. My Mom told me what a brave boy I had been and she and Dad took me to Connors' for a treat on the way home!

Chapter Twenty-Four
Favorite Toys

07/31/15

As a child, I often received a toy or some other gift that I would tend to like more than the others. None of these "treasures" were very expensive, but as a child, they held some sort of magic for me. One Christmas, when I was 4 or 5, I received a "Handy Andy" carpenter's tool set from Santa. It came in a nice, rectangular case with a buckle-like closure. There was a picture of a small boy dressed in carpenter's overalls holding a hammer and a handsaw on the top. Inside there was a small "hand" saw with very dull teeth, a small hammer, a plane, a screwdriver, a small adjustable wrench, and a pair of pliers. The metal parts were painted with a powder blue finish. I loved this gift because, by that time, my Dad was working as a carpenter and I used to "pretend" to be helping him when he would have a project going on in the basement workshop. I remember being very proud of my little tool set and I would often show it to my friends when they were around. One time, in the late spring, my Dad was talking to Sam Kuhn in the street in front of Rusiska's house. His son Vic came out to play with me so I went and got my wood plane to show him. His dad began complimenting me on my tool and Vic got jealous and upset. He took the plane from me and threw it down the street, where it landed with a metallic crash. I was sad and Vic got into trouble as the plane was now cracked and unusable. I remember my Dad telling Mr. Kuhn that it was OK, but I sure didn't feel that way.

Another time, Mrs. Maglott was selling small knick-knacks from her dining room table, to earn extra money. She was connected to a vendor that sold these types of trinkets wholesale to her. My birthday was coming soon and my Mom went to Mrs. Maglotts' "store" and bought me a plastic ship-in-a-bottle kit and a very small metal miniature six shooter that came in a little vinyl holster. The gun was no more than an inch and a half in length, but it was highly detailed and had a working hammer and trigger! I used to sit in the living room of our house on rainy days and play with that gun until it finally broke. The ship in a bottle came with some sort of plastic glue and my Mom let me put it together by myself. It actually came out pretty well, but I had smeared the glue on the clear plastic bottle so it did have the markings of a 5 or 6-year-old fabricator! Mom kept the ship in the cupboard above the telephone in the kitchen for a long time, but it too disappeared into the ether of time. I must have had an affinity for miniature toys because another of my favorite playthings was a large bag of miniature plastic airplanes that were from different eras up to the new jet age, that my Mom probably bought at Woolworths. I especially liked the "double wingers", and the newest jet models. I would play with them for hours on end. I liked jets so much that I would ask my Mom to bring me books on them whenever she would go to the mobile library (which was weekly).

Favorite Toys

My friends and I would sometimes ride our bikes around Harvard and Tudor Avenues pretending that we were on various airplanes that we saw in a book that Joe Henney owned. It was a special time in America. A gift that I received when I was 10 or 11 years old was a "Fanner .50" revolver that had a holster and removable "dummy" bullets that you could load with "Greenie Stick'em Caps"! This was the era of many Western TV shows, and MATTEL, the toy manufacturer, bought this toy to market with much television fanfare. Every boy wanted one! I was lucky enough to be one of them!! One fall, my Dad brought home a full-sized football for me. It must have been around 1953 or 1954. I say this because it was a model "autographed" by Johnny Lattner who played for Notre Dame (my Dad's favorite team), and who won the Heisman trophy in 1953. The only problem with the ball was that it was white with black bands and it was a full-sized model, which was huge to me back then. I never got much use out of it as I could hardly carry the ball, and my friends had no interest in using it. I will say that for all his other shortcomings, my Dad always bought me things that he felt were neat and that I would like. They were often excellent choices!

Chapter Twenty-Five
Stout's Grocery Market et. al.

08/18/15

Back in the early 1950s and into the early 1960s, things weren't as automated as they are today. More people were at work doing things like delivering bread and milk to their customers around the city. Back then, we would wait for our OMAR bread man to drive up to our house, bounce out of his truck, and run up to our front door where my Mom would give him an order for bread and other assorted baked goods. Large stores and shopping centers such as West Park were in their infancy. We also had ISALY'S milk products delivered weekly to a little, galvanized, and insulated, milk box which sat on our breezeway apron next to the south side of the house. "ISLAY'S" was written on the front of the milk box in a large, dark red script. Back then, milk came in glass bottles that were sealed with little, round cardboard tops. In the winter, my Mom would scramble, when she heard the sound of the milkman rattling the bottles, to get them into the house before the milk started to freeze. If it did freeze, the little tops would pop off the bottles and milk would run into the milk box! Later, in the sixties, we would wait for the

CHARLES CHIP man to drive up in his brownish-yellow colored truck. If we had the money, we could order a can of barbecue chips or other snack items that would come to sit on top of our refrigerator in the kitchen.

If we kids had money, we would usually head down to Connors' Westgate Pantry to buy our candy. There was a little, cute Italian lady with a wonderfully sunny disposition, who worked part-time for the Connors named Annie Ross. She was the mother of our St. Peter's friends Jim and Charlie Ross who lived across Park Avenue West on Oxford Avenue. She was always behind the soda fountain at the store and would greet us with a cheerful "hello" when we would arrive. My Mom was always in awe of Annie because she had the most beautiful smile, with the brightest sparkling white teeth. One time, Mom asked her how she came to have such beautiful teeth. Annie replied that, when she was young, if she felt that one of her teeth was not coming in straight, she would apply pressure to it with her finger. After that, whether or not she was telling the truth, I would push on mine for the same reason! Perhaps it helped? Some of my favorite candies were Necco Wafers and JuJuBe's. I especially liked the licorice-flavored wafers and would often trade other flavors with my friends who weren't as fond of licorice. Sky, Zero, Clark, and Seven Up bars were also in the "favorites" category for me. It's a wonder that I have any teeth at all!

Across Grasmere Avenue, to the west, stood an early grocery store called Stouts' Market. When I was very young (probably 3 or 4), I remember walking down Harvard Avenue to Tudor Street and then through the Harvard extension with my Mom to do grocery shopping. The store fronted on Park Avenue West and I remember it was built of cinder blocks painted in bright white and on the inside was painted in bright pastel colors. I remember little else about Stouts Market other than that it had small rectangular windows placed high up in the rear (south) of the store, where sunlight would stream in, illuminating half of the building! It also had an early checkout at the front of the store that had an automated, aluminum conveyor belt that directed the groceries to the bagging area. Lastly, my favorite memory was that one time, when we were in the cereal aisle, I spotted a box of cereal called "Jets". Back then, the jet age was in full bloom and I loved seeing jets scream in the air!! There were no laws prohibiting many things (as there are today, unfortunately) and sonic booms could be heard fairly often when we were at play. They were scary but thrilling to experience! I wanted a box of the "Jets" cereal, and I do believe my Mom relented and bought them for me. I can't remember whether I liked them, but I do remember that I was disappointed in them as the cereal had no resemblance to a jet. They were little round, yellowish-white balls! Ah, modern marketing...In 1953, the Marathon Oil Company of Findlay, Ohio purchased Stouts' Market and built a Marathon gas service station in its place. The owner was Fred Gertel, who ran it with his son, Fred, Jr. until well into the late 1970s.

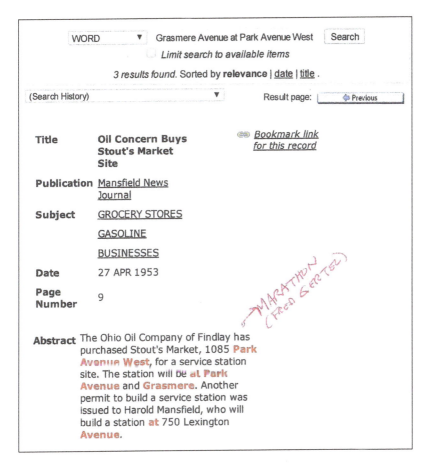

Memorandum of the purchase of Stout's property by the Marathon Oil Company Of Findlay, Ohio

Other treats delivered to us at home were from Bloodgood's Ice Cream Company. They would hire teenagers to pedal around the city on assigned routes on bicycles that had a white, insulated freezer chest attached between two, large front tires. The chest had Bloodgood's emblazoned across the front of the chest and a menu of items and prices on the sides. The teens rode behind the chest where they would pedal and they would ring little silver bells that were attached to the handle of the ice cream chest. The sound of the bells would send us kids into a flurry of excitement and we would yell "The ice cream man is coming" and then beg our parents for change to buy a summer treat! My favorites were the ice cream sandwich (10 cents) and the double popsicles (7 cents). I remember I sometimes felt sorry for the teens, especially on very hot summer days, as they would struggle to pedal the heavy freezer up the incline on our street.

Chapter Twenty-Six
Cindy Lou Who, and Other Pets

08/19/15

Our new neighborhood was inundated with post-WWII children, the "baby boomers". This also meant that there were quite a few pets, mostly canines, that went along with those families. We had Sparky, who met an untimely demise on Park Avenue West around 1953. We didn't have another pet, other than a few goldfish my Mom would buy me on our trips to F.W. Woolworths, and several ill-fated bunnies (they all died) that our Dad brought home for us, for the next few years. Then, in 1960, a dog my sister Susan named Cindy, came to live in our house. Cindy was a near full-bred Manchester Terrier. She was all black except for a white chest and a white paw or two. She was so small when Dad brought her home that she would fit into one of my Dad's size 8 shoes (and Dad had small feet!), where she would occasionally hide. She became our friend, a survivor, and on occasion, our embarrassment. You see, she had a long love affair with a male "friend", who lived up on Grasmere Avenue named Jiggs. Jiggs was a beautiful, white Spitz breed with a wonderful curly tail. He was majestic! They had at least three litters together and this provided us kids with a real-life education on the birds and the bees! We watched Cindy having her litter in our basement, totally enthralled and mystified by the proceedings. We kept one or two of the puppies, notably "Supercar" and "Ginger", named by my sister Susan, because of his tan and white coat. Susan could get Cindy all excited by just saying "Jiggs, Cindy, Jiggs"! Cindy was a friend and a comfort to all seven of us Adamescu kids for the next 18 years. She passed away in 1978, and my brother Pack buried her with full honors in front of the apple tree in the backyard. This was near the woods and Pack lovingly made a cross for her marker. Mr. and Mrs. King, who lived on Harvard extension, had a beautiful collie named "Lady". Sherree Wilson had a beautiful Labrador Retriever that she would parade up and down the street. Mr. and Mrs. Lake, who also lived on Harvard extension, had two yappy, but darling, Pomeranians.

Mr. and Mrs. Wycoff lived up Harvard Avenue from us and had a huge German Shepherd named "Wolf". Their kids were Nancy, Curt, and David. Nancy was a couple of years older than me, Curt was two years younger but one of my good friends, and Davey was my brother Jim's age. Wolf was the closest thing to a full-sized wolf as he could possibly be, without actually being one! The only person that could handle him was Mr. Wycoff (Willard) and he was a Purple Heart veteran who was a paratrooper in WWII! To be fair, Wolf was kept chained up in all kinds of weather, behind the Wycoff's house, near the woods, in a doghouse. I believe this is why he had such a bad disposition. He was MEAN! You could hear him howling at any time of day, and he had a ferocious bark that was more than menacing. As kids, we were warned to stay away from him at all times! One year, Mrs. Wycoff (Gerry) was the Cub Scout den mother for Curt and his friends. In the spring, during a scout meeting at the Wycoff house, Wolf was barking furiously at the scouts. Mrs. Wycoff went out to quiet Wolf and was attacked! She suffered numerous wounds and was taken to the emergency room by a neighbor. Unfortunately, the scouts witnessed the attack. Mr. Wycoff was called home from Weidner Pontiac and had Wolf put down. Mrs. Wycoff eventually healed and was fine, but there was never another dog at the Wyckoff house after that. Overall, there were many other pets around and our neighborhood was one of constant pet and stray activity!

Chapter Twenty-Seven

Television, Our New Wonderful Gadget

09/29/15

As kids, we were part of a new generation of entertainment, brought to us through the new medium of television. Radio was on its way out as the number one information tool. In the early fifties, my parents had a Philco black and white console television that sat in the southeast corner of our living room. Back then, TV reception came through an antenna placed, most often, on the roof. Ours was connected to the chimney as well as to a box that sat on top of the TV. This box was called a "Tenna Rotor", and was attached to the TV through a "lead in" wire. The "Tenna Rotor" would allow you to turn the antenna for better reception from the comfort of your living room. The face of the "Tenna Rotor" was similar to the face of a compass, and one could turn the antenna in the direction of the stations you wanted to receive, by turning the dial to the compass heading desired. It would make a "thump, thump, thump" sound as it zeroed in on the stations. We were able to get channel 3 (KYW), channel 5 (WEWS) which was the oldest station in Ohio (it began broadcasting in 1948), and channel 8 (WJW) from Cleveland on most days, but if the weather was inclement, the stations would come in fuzzy. When college football games were on, Dad would turn the antenna toward Columbus, Ohio, to pick up Notre Dame games when they were not broadcast on Cleveland TV. Eventually, the Tenna Rotor "gave up the ghost" and Dad would climb up on the roof to turn the antenna with a pipe wrench. This job fell to me in time when I was old enough. I would wait by the open south window next to the TV set and give Dad feedback when the reception was clearest by yelling "That's good!" Whenever the TV went on the "fritz" (which seemed to be often) Dad would call Ed Odson, our TV repairman, who lived out on South Main Street hill. This was before the highway system was started and South Main Street became part of U.S. Route 71.

Saturday morning TV became dedicated to children's programming. We had so many choices starting around 7:00 am with the sign-on of the station. Back then, stations would sign off at midnight with the playing of our national anthem and sign on at 6:00 or 7:00 am. In the interim, the screen would turn to "snow" until a "test pattern", a fixed picture used by the station's TV engineers to adjust the transmission of the picture, would appear. Early Saturday morning would begin with shows like "Albert P Worm", "Mighty Mouse", "Howdy Doody", "Heckle and Jeckle", "Kukla, Fran and Ollie", "Winky Dink and You", "Soupy Sales", as well as many others, too many to name. Later in the morning and early afternoon on Saturdays, we would watch "Circus Boy" (my sister Jeanne was in love with the Circus Boy character played by Mickey Dolenz, later of the "Monkees"), "Big Top", "The Lone Ranger", "Tales of Texas Rangers" (one of my early favorites), "Sky King", "Fury", and the assorted Roy Rogers and Dale Evans movie shorts. Pat Brady was the star who played a character that owned the cantankerous "Nellie Belle", a WWII vintage Jeep. I'm sure that Susan and Jeanne had their favorites as well. We certainly never had a lack of something to watch and entertain us back in the 50s!

Television was up and coming in our lives (for better or worse), but we also enjoyed some of the wonderful children's movies of the time at our local theaters. These films were often by Walt Disney, at either the Madison, Ohio, or Park theaters, which were all within walking distance of one another in downtown Mansfield. I remember our neighbor, Helen Rusiska, driving us kids to see a very early 1950s movie, starring Lucille Ball and Desi Arnaz, called "The Long, Long Trailer" at the Ohio and later, "Lady and the Tramp" at the Madison Theatre. This would have been around 1954 or 1955. During the mornings before I started school, I loved to watch "Ding Dong School" with Miss Frances. Her show would open with her ringing an old-fashioned school bell, beckoning us to come to school. She was a kind, matronly woman who would give us lessons on life and teach us how to write letters and color. One year, she offered these crayon-type products that she used on the show, for sale via the mail. I convinced my Mom to place an order for them, and she did! They arrived in a nice little box and I remember that they were of a large diameter so that they would be easy for a small child to use. The neat thing about these crayons was that they could be used to color in a coloring book like a regular crayon, but they were also formulated so that they could be dipped in water and used as a watercolor "brush"! I remember that my sister Susan and I must have been very messy with them as my Mom would keep them in our bedroom in a closet high on a shelf, and only let us use them if she had the time to supervise us, which wasn't all that often.

Chapter Twenty-Eight
Our Family Automobile Early History

09/30/15

Cars played a large part in my early childhood memories. I still vividly remember riding in my parent's 1947 Pontiac Streamliner. This was the car that my parents bought after returning home from WWII and before they were married in February of 1947. It was a four-door sedan and had a really nice interior with brownish-tan striped cloth seats that kept you warm on cold winter days. It was painted a "Mariner Blue" on the bottom half and a "Silverwing Grey" on the roof, hood, and trunk. Two-tone painted cars were beginning to be the rage then, running well into the 50s, and I still like them to this day. My Dad also had a 1930 Chevrolet two-door sedan which I remember was almost always parked in the garage. It was painted black and had wire wheels with a spare wheel hanging from the rear of the car. I don't ever remember riding in it, although I may have, but I used to crawl around on it from time to time. It had running boards that allowed me to step up and open the door. Inside there was a long, floor-mounted stick shifter, a metal clutch, brake, and gas pedals. I faintly remember a glass vase (for flowers?) hanging from the dash as well. The roof of the Chevy was made of a heavy canvas top that I remember my Dad would patch with some sort of tar in a can. It seemed that the roof would leak when it rained hard enough! I also remember my Dad telling someone that the suspension was getting so bad that he was beginning to hit his head on the roof from bouncing, whenever he would drive over a large bump in the road. I think the Chevy was sold somewhere in the early 50s, as I don't remember it much past that time. After the Chevy was sold, there was a succession of work cars that came into my Dad's possession. The first I remember was a used 1948 Buick 2-door "Sedanette" that my Dad bought from our new neighbors to the north, the Gardners. I was probably 4 or 5 at the time. It was a washed-out green color and we didn't keep it for very long. When Don Gardner sold the Buick to my Dad (this remembrance was from my dear Mom), he forgot to mention that the floor was almost completely rusted through! I don't know if Dad made Don Gardner take the car back or if he just sold it or junked it, but it wasn't around for very long in our driveway!

After the Buick, Dad purchased a used 1949 Pontiac 2-door sedan, also in a washed-out green color, from Weidner Pontiac. This car I remember a little better. The thing that is still imprinted in my mind is the Indian Chief hood ornament. I remember it because the face of the "Chief" for Pontiac was in an orange translucent plastic, which fascinated me no end! Another thing I remember is that this car had a Hydramatic transmission, meaning that this car didn't need to be shifted manually, it shifted automatically on its own. It had a really cool-looking sun visor on the outside and had a special magnifying traffic light viewer on the left side of the dash, that allowed the driver to "see" the traffic light, even though the sun visor would normally block the view. In the late 50s, when our family had reached 6 children, my Dad and Mom purchased a used 1956 red Ford Country Squire station wagon from their friends, the Schwartz's, who lived down in Lexington, Ohio. This was a nice used car and it served us for several years, mostly because it could carry nine passengers. I remember the rearmost seat by the tailgate that faced backward, which was a thrill to us kids, but I'm sure would never pass in this day and age for safety reasons. Also, in the late 50s, my Dad bought the coolest car that we would ever own as a family! It was a 1955 Pontiac 2-door Star Chief that Dad and Mom bought from Mr. Massa. Mr. Massa also had a large family and probably sold the car because he too needed a larger vehicle. The car was a two-toned color with "Driftwood beige" on the bottom and "Polo white" on top. It had leather seats, a gorgeous interior and it had a first for Pontiacs, a V-8 engine! It was a beautiful car, but like all the cars my parents were able to afford after the 1947 Streamliner, it was used. This meant Dad was always forced to fix or have someone else repair the car. Often, he would be without a car, until he could have it fixed. The mechanics he could afford tended to be a mixed bag of professional and backyard mechanics. The results were often mixed as well. This caused friction between my Mom and Dad for many reasons. My Mom wasn't as tolerant as my Dad about who repaired the cars and the results that followed, which would occasionally lead to a fight between them. Ah well...

Chapter Twenty-Nine

My Father Bought Two Bikes for Me

10/01/15

I owned two bikes in my youth. The first was a small red 20" Shelby bicycle my Dad purchased for me and then helped me to ride. When I was old enough to learn, we would start in the middle of our front yard, with Dad steadying the bike for me, and then he would guide me down the little hill next to Gardner's driveway and give me a little push out onto Harvard Avenue. Before long, I eventually got the hang of it, and soon I was riding on my own! Each spring, I would drag the bike out of the garage and ride it around on the street. Back then, in the winter, they would spread cinders on the street instead of salt. There would always be a little residue of the cinders in the gutters on the side of the road in the spring, and if I would fall from my little bike, I remember getting them ground into my knees or elbows. My Mom would rescue me by washing my wounds and applying mercurochrome to the site. Mercurochrome was always the fallback cure for any scrape or burn back then. It didn't sting and it was a reddish-orange color, which would stain our skin for a few days. Mercurochrome, along with sulfa tablets that Mom would bring home from her work as a Registered Nurse at Mansfield General Hospital, and band-aids, was the extent of our home medicine chest. Sulfa was the precursor to penicillin, and all of us kids took it, until the late 50s, when we had a fever.

When I was around 10 or 11, my Dad bought me an English bike from Al Bechtel who lived up the street from us on Harvard Avenue. It belonged to his son, Alan, who was 5 or 6 years older than me, and was beginning to drive a car. It was a beautiful bike manufactured by the Invicta Company in the United Kingdom. It had the thin English type of tires with tan sidewalls, 3-speed Sturmey Archer gears, dual hand brakes, and was a dark reddish maroon color. I rode that bike until I started driving and I customized it in the early sixties with "monkey bar" handlebars. My friends and I would take long bike trips around the area. Kenny Rusiska owned a Schwinn "Corvette" Bike and we would often ride out to Trimble Road and then down to Millsboro Road until we got to Home Road, and then left to the deer park near Lexington, and back again. In the fall, we would stop on Millsboro Road next to a field of "hog" corn and pick a few ears that we would take back to his garage, and rub the kernels off, in preparation for Halloween. I remember getting blisters for my efforts! The area around our neighborhood was just gorgeous back then! We were still surrounded by farms, the geography was hilly, surrounded by wooded areas and forests, that were beautiful year-round, but extraordinarily so in the autumn! The trees were always ablaze with the prettiest, most breathtaking colors! The crisp clean smell of the countryside was always near. We were able to burn leaves back then, which had a wonderful scent that I will never forget!!

Chapter Thirty

The Beautiful Woods, Listening to Helen

01/25/16

The woods behind our house were always open to new adventures for us, especially as a child. In the spring, the smell of the woods with the scent of the good rich soil, would slowly build with the passing of each new day. The scent of winter ending would collide with the new smells of spring in the air! A new day would dawn bright with the sun slowly rising from the east where it spent the winter, to a higher position in the west where it would remain, almost overhead, throughout the summer. With this movement came longer days, increasing bit by bit until June 21st (the summer solstice), until it would remain light until almost 10:00 pm! I remember June 21st because that's my birthday and it's the longest day of the year! Spring was time for new explorations in the woods. We would hunt for new places to put a treehouse, or discover new places to explore that we hadn't seen before in our many hikes through the woods. Spring was always "iffy" as we would wear our coats and shoes early in the day, but we might have taken them off by afternoon, as the heat would build up from the sun rising in the sky. Spring was a wonderful time! Grandpa Adamescu would be out spading his new garden, Dad would be starting a new job somewhere, Mom would be busy with spring cleaning, and all of us kids would be straining "at the bit" to be off on a new adventure to someplace unknown!

Such an adventure took place one early spring day when Susan, Kenny Rusiska, and I were off in search of new things to explore. We were only 6 or 7 years old and Helen (Kenny's mom) told us not to go too far into the woods to keep clean. We managed to keep her instruction pretty close to heart as we explored the top of the forest close to our homes. We had a good time as we searched the forest for interesting things such as squirrels busily hunting for treasures they had stored in the ground and the return of birds from their southern homes. We also looked at the carvings in the trees to see who had put them there. Being only in the second grade didn't help us much, but we found a few and were happy with that piece of luck. We were dressed rather warmly as it was overcast and we had on boots, hats, and our winter coats. That's when we decided it was time to explore further our search for new things. I don't remember who decided what, but before we knew it we were heading down the embankment towards the lower regions of the woods, the place we were forbidden to visit by Helen! Kenny knew that his mother would be upset if she found us down there and so he told Susan and me to be very quiet, words that eventually would be forgotten. One thing led to another and sooner than later we ventured into a pool of water that was filled every season, by the snow that melted from the warming weather. When I said "ventured into a pool", I meant it! Before you knew what was happening, Susan, Kenny, and I were ankle-deep in the water! Susan's one boot came off in the muddy water! We enjoyed ourselves playing in the water and were having a good time, until somewhere in the distance we heard "Kenneth, Kenneth " and immediately recognized Helen's voice as she called her son. Well, we were slightly panicked! We became more panicked as Helen appeared at the top of the hill and said, "Kenneth, you get up here this instant, you're gonna get a lickin' as soon as you do! Johnny and Susan, you better get home, your Mom is going to be mad at you for what you did!" Kenny hurried up the hill to Helen who gave him a quick brush to the side of his head. Susan and I hurried up the hill to an angry Helen who told us to go home immediately. We did, but thankfully to a Mom that was happy, we were home safely (even though she was a little bit peeved!)

Chapter Thirty-One
My Friend, Stanley Popp

02/05/2016

When I was very young, one of the first of my playmates was Stanley Popp, who lived across the street from me. Stan was a nice boy who loved to watch his Dad build things, as his job was as a carpenter. My Dad told me that Mr. Popp actually built their house with his own hands, an unusual feat of the times. Stan had two sisters, Gayleen and Joy. Gayleen was older and the boys in the neighborhood gathered around her when she was around, as she was beautiful! I didn't notice the beautiful part and I imagine the older boys didn't notice quite as much as I thought they did, but they were around often when Gayleen was about! Joy was only a toddler, but I recollect a story about her and a coloring book in her living room. It seems as though she was being pesky and bothering us older kids to no end by standing there complaining that she too wanted to color in the book. Well, I got mad at her and pushed her away from the coloring book, and she stumbled and fell on top of the crayon container top. Now, back then, Mrs. Popp used a coffee can, which held the crayons neatly inside. However, the top of the coffee can also had very sharp edges, as most of the cans did back then. In order to get the can open, the user would have to take the attached key, which would be connected to the can, and use it to remove the top. This left a knife-like edge to the top, and wouldn't you know it, that's what Joy fell on as I pushed her away from the coloring book! Her knee started bleeding and she started crying! Mrs. Popp came rushing in and was looking for the culprit who had done the pushing. I remember saying, out of fear, that I had pushed her slightly, but that she stumbled and fell. Susan and Stan seemed to be no wiser, so I let it stand that I had pushed her slightly. Such are the wages of sin, as I never told anyone the "real" reason for her fall!

Stan and his sisters were a member of a family that had very strong Christian beliefs, and therefore, had certain parental "restrictions" placed upon them. One of the most visible signs of their Christian heritage was that they didn't believe in getting a lot of Christmas presents. This always bothered me, because I liked Stan, and I couldn't understand the big difference between getting a lot of gifts and getting nearly none. This was borne out completely one Christmas, probably when we were 5 or 6, as I was visiting Stan and asked him what he'd gotten for Christmas. He told me, very matter of fact, that he'd gotten a child's version of a shaving kit. When I asked him "Really?", he responded "Yes". At the time, I couldn't understand what he meant, but as the years went on it became much clearer to me. You see, they were just good Christian kids!

One other thing I remember about Stan was that his Dad drove an early 1950s Ford. This was a nice car to be driven at that time and he spared no expense buying that Ford in the early fifties! It was dark blue in color and was a four-door sedan and although the Popps lived very frugally, they looked very sharp in their newer Ford!!

Chapter Thirty-Two
Life Up at the Rusiska's New House

09/09/2121

I was 7 or 8 years old when the Rusiskas' moved to the top of Harvard Avenue in 1956 (their new address was 165 Harvard Avenue). They bought their lot from a man named Mr. Brumenshenkel. It was on the east side of the street and abutted the fence to the Black Estates on the south side of the house. It was a glorious lot! They had a big backyard that lent itself to be used as a baseball field when we were a little older (and when their mother, Helen, wasn't banning us from using it). Helen was afraid that we would break their large picture window that was in the new house, just about where the third base would be located.

When they moved into their new house, I began to get my introduction to "rock n roll" music! At 7 or 8 years old, we would go to Kenny and Bob's bedroom at the rear of the house, and listen to records that George Sr. and Georgie Jr. had bought for the family. We listened to the Everly Brothers sing "Bye, Bye Love" and "Little Susie." There was also Jimmy Rodgers, who sang "Honeycomb", which was one of my favorites! Elvis sang "Don't

Be Cruel," and "Hound Dog", which I thought was an amazing song. As well as the 'Platters', who sang "The Great Pretender". One of the funniest records that we listened to was "The Flying Saucer," parts I and II, which recorded several big hits of the day, and then remixed them to a funny story about a flying saucer that was landing on Earth! We listened to that record dozens of times over the next 10 years! The Rusiska house was the one place I learned about hit records!

When I would go up to the Rusiska household and it was cold or rainy outside, we would normally go down to their basement to play. One side of the basement was finished and had a beautiful fireplace, the other side of the basement wasn't finished and had a model H.O. railroad train setup mounted on a ping-pong table. We played all types of games as we sat in the room with the fireplace. We played "Risk", "Yahtzee", "Life" and various card games. During the beginning of the Beatles era, we listened to the Beatles records. When we would play in the other room, we would play with the trains and assorted things that went with them. One thing I distinctly remember was the little yellow freight train that was faster than all the other trains, and I would drive it around the track as fast as I could until it fell off the tracks!

During the summer we would play wiffle ball in the small field to the north of the Rusiskas. We spent one summer clearing out the field so that we could use it for wiffle ball. The lot still belonged to Mr. Brumenshenkel, but he never checked on it. We used Georgie's small Jacobsen tractor and trailer and, as I remember, it came out very nicely.

Lots of games were played there during the summer with all of our neighborhood friends who liked baseball, and even George Sr. would occasionally join us!

Chapter Thirty-Three
The Adamescu's Early Trip to Niagara Falls

09/01/2021

When I was about 4 or 5 years old, my Mom and Dad took Susan and I, along with our Grandpa and Grandma Adamescu, on a road trip to upstate New York, to see the beautiful Niagara Falls. This is where my Dad took my Mom on their honeymoon in the 1947 Pontiac Streamliner. This was after their wedding at St. Peter's Church in Mansfield.

I remember the trip was sunny and we had a very nice ride in the wide seats of the 1947 Pontiac Streamliner. I remember that when we had to use the bathroom, my Dad would pull the car off the road, and we would relieve ourselves on the side of the two-lane road with cars zipping by us. By the way, highways were in the future in this part of the country, so we made the trip on the narrow 2 lane roads the whole way up from Mansfield.

The Adamescu's Early Trip to Niagara Falls

The wedding picture of Great Uncle Herbert and Grandma Emma, my Mom and Dad, and Grandpa and Grandma Adamescu

The 1947 Pontiac didn't have air conditioning back then, so toward the end of the trip we were getting very hot and clammy in the car. I remember Grandpa Adamescu was getting very hot and was complaining to my Dad in Romanian about his level of discomfort (actually, we were all getting uncomfortable at this point) but my Dad persisted and we made it to the falls in about 7 hours. On the way up, my Dad stopped at a roadside store, and my Mom bought a supply of the orange sherbet that came in a circular cardboard container, with a hard paper push stick at the bottom. I remember that the cardboard container had a group of clowns drawn in color on the outside of the package and we welcomed them with open arms! I remember that I didn't like the orange sherbet very much, but I ate the whole thing down to the hard paper stick in a few minutes!!

When we arrived at Niagara Falls, we watched all the people who were there and the magnificent Falls as they cascaded over and down to the large, tremendous splashes of water at the bottom! I remember the area of shops around the Falls was brightly colored and there were a group of shops that had souvenirs and candy in them. We had a grand time!! After seeing the Falls from the top, my Mom and Dad took us downstairs, to a giant tunnel that ran under the Falls, and bought us each a ticket to ride on the ferry boats, which circled at the bottom. We were each given a raincoat to wear. On the way down the stone stairs, we were able to stop about halfway, to see Niagara Falls cascading down towards us and getting thoroughly soaked! I remember Susan and I were afraid of the Falls during this part of the trip, but we prevailed and made it down to the ferry boats. I remember the name on the side of our boat was "The Maid of the Mist" and it certainly lived up to its name! It was starting to rain during this part of the trip, and we were literally getting soaked by the rain and the Falls! The ferry boat ride was a grand adventure, moving in near the crashing waterfalls and then pulling out away from them! When we left Niagara Falls, Susan and I were very tired and we drove home asleep in the 1947 Pontiac (I think Mom and Grandma Adamescu were sleeping too). Dad had to stay awake to drive as Mom wouldn't get her driver's license until 1956.

Chapter Thirty-Four
The Woods, My First Big Treehouse, Learning a Lesson

09/02/2021

Another memory I have of my time on Harvard Avenue was of building tree houses in the woods in the back of our house. We were living in an era where a "no cut" law of the trees in the woods was in force. There were trees 200-300 years old living in the back! The Schroeder part of the woods ran from Park Avenue West south to the middle of our property, and a virgin forest in the rest of the wooded areas, which ran to Millsboro Road and beyond. I was very young when Dad took me back into the woods, and I remember all the foliage, trees, streams, hills, and other bits of nature when we would go back. There were tall pines, beech, maple, hickory, elm, chestnut, oak, and all kinds of weeds and brush. The streams ran from north to south, and a couple of them ended up in pools of water in the spring and summer. As we grew a little older, my friends and I started to think of all the tree houses we might be able to build in the woods! My first tree house was built along with

Kenny Rusiska. We happened to notice a very large birch tree, located about forty feet in the back of our property line. It was about 40" in diameter! We were 12 or 13 years old. Since my Dad was a carpenter, he had all the tools we would need to construct our masterpiece! We started our search for supplies at Home Materials, in their scrap yard, located in a large metal bin behind the store. Home Materials was located at the base of Harvard Extension, fronting Park Avenue West. It was about 1,000 feet beyond my house. We were living in the post-WWII neighborhood where everything was built very close to our residence. We gathered what we thought was enough wood to cover our tree house and headed back home through the woods. As we started our build, we found out that we didn't have enough 2" x 4" (two by fours) to build a set of steps up to our fort. At this point, I decided to hunt through Dad's collection of wood located in our basement. I got sidelined by looking at all the tools he had and decided we could use a saw, a measuring tape, and an assortment of nails to go along with the hammer I had borrowed earlier. I soon found out how wrong my assumptions had been, as my Dad was not inclined, in the least, to have us use his equipment. But, I'll continue with my story. Alas, he had no 2" x 4" wood in the basement, so we decided to build our steps out of the 1" x 4" siding that we found in the metal bin. As time wore on and we used our tree fort many times, we discovered that this wasn't the best choice for steps, as all the 1" x 4" steps wore out rather quickly and disintegrated. We were constantly on the lookout for 2" x 4" steps to replace the 1" x 4" steps. When we finally reached the top of our fort, which was about 20 feet in the air, we used ¾" plywood and some flooring boards to cover the floor. The floor was about 4' x 6' and was just big enough for a comfortable fit for Kenny and me.

As we finished the work on our tree fort, many of our friends began working on their version of a tree house. This continued until my brother Pack, and his friends, the Constantinatus boys, built a magnificent tree house of their own that was big enough to be featured by Bob Simon** in a full-page Mansfield News Journal story! My brother Pack was 11 years younger than I was, so he was probably 13 years old when they built their tree fort. I would have been 24 years old when that happened!

I have a quick story to tell you about our tree fort. Kenny and I were in our tree house just wasting away time when my sister Susan began calling me from our house.

Well, we figured this would be a good time to hide from her, so we laid down flat on the floor of our tree fort, in what we felt was a good hiding place. Susan and her friend Connie Gardner kept calling us and they decided that we must be up in our place in the birch tree. Well, they came back and looked up in our fort and Susan started screaming for my Mom! She ran toward the house screaming that I was hurt and lying unconscious in the tree fort! Our attempt at hiding was in vain and my Mom came back out to the birch tree. Kenny and I were saying "Here we are!" My Mom said (and I think I'm quoting her verbatim), "John, you should be ashamed of yourself! Making your sister think you were hurt and having her come screaming for me!" I tried to answer her by saying we were hiding from her, but that fell upon deaf ears…Well, that's my story…

**(Bob Simon was an award-winning News Journal writer and a friend of my Mom.)

When Susan and Jim Konves were dating (before they were married in 1974), he wrote a story about them, which also included romantic pictures of them walking in the snow at the Mansfield Branch of The Ohio State University.)

Chapter Thirty-Five

John Learns Another Lesson, A Robot Attack From Next Door

09/03/2021

One of the stories that showed my lack of early self-confidence and my Mother's abundance of "pull yourself up by the bootstraps" confidence, came one summer when I was 6 or 7 years old. I have already told you of the ravine that fell at the corner of our street, and how we kids used to play down there many times. Well, I was not a confident child when I was 6 or 7 years old, and I caused quite a scene for my playmates. The hill down to the bottom of the ravine was steep (although at that age it was very steep to me), and my friends were telling me to climb down the hill. They were already doing this, so I summoned up my courage to attempt the same thing. I got down on my belly and started to crawl down the embankment backward. I got about two or three steps behind me and all of a sudden it struck!! I was full of fright on the way down and I started to whimper to my friends to help me! I just couldn't move! My friends went up the street to my house and got my Mom to help me out of the predicament in which I found myself. My Mom came down to the ravine in a slow trot and she looked down at me and started to speak. Now, I was kind of expecting a nice, sympathetic, "let's get you out of there" spoken word from my Mom. She was always looking out for me. My Mom spoke the following to me, and I quote, "Johnny, get yourself out of there! It isn't that steep and you are being a little child. Now come on and get up here!" She had a look of disappointment on her face. I was shocked by her non-sympathetic words and I struggled to get myself out of my predicament. I grabbed three handfuls of dirt in my effort. The first was just dirt and grass. The second was a little more dirt and grass, and the third was enough to finally pull myself up and out! Ah, Moms...

When I was 8 or 9 years old, our new neighbors who moved in next to us were the Kirkpatricks (the Rusiskas moved up the street in 1956). The mother of the Kirkpatricks was a permanent resident of the house and her children, who were missionaries in Africa, would often visit her for long periods when they were back in the United States.

Their son, Bob, would often stay with his grandmother while his parents were in Africa. Bob was approximately 5 or 6 years older than me and became an "older brother" and we became friendly over time. There was also a young man, Alan Bechtel, who lived up the street from me, who was in the same grade in high school as Bob. They had a project to come up with an item for their science class, which I won't describe right now. Well, both Bob and Alan were quite intelligent and they came up with a "doozy" of a project!! Bob was friendly with my parents and he told them of their creation, which they would spring on me at night to get the full effect! Well, my parents got the message and played their parts to great effect! One night, during the summer, it was dark and my parents began saying "Look towards the Kirkpatrick house!" in an excited manner! So I looked out the screen towards their house and what do you think I saw? It was a life-sized robot that was lit up and was moving towards our house! At first, I was a little scared, but as soon as they got nearer to our house, I saw that Bob was behind the robot, who was actually Allan, guiding him along the way! He had the robot over his head and down to his waist, and was walking in a modified robot way, to give the appearance of a real robot!

As previously mentioned, Dad later bought Allan's bike for me, an Invicta 26" in red color, and I enjoyed it for many years to come. Bob and I would have a few adventures in electronics, in Bob's basement, also over the next couple of years.

Chapter Thirty-Six
Little Georgie Rusiska

09/07/2021

When Susan and I were very young, about 3 and 2, we always had numerous friends to play with. One of the first of these friends was Georgie Rusiska who lived one door south of us at 84 Harvard Avenue. I don't have clear memories of that time as Georgie was a couple of years older than I was (he was 5 years old). However, my Mom had a picture, probably taken by Helen (Georgie's Mom), of the three of us riding my little tricycle in our front yard! Georgie was steering, Susan was being held by my Mom on the seat in front of me, and I was riding on the little platform on the back of the tricycle! My Mom was very young and had a big smile on her face!

Little Georgie Rusiska

My Mom holding Susan, Georgie Rusiska, and me riding my tricycle

I remember another story about Georgie in the summer that showed his kind of humor! I had just had my 4th birthday and had gotten a tube of the toy of the '50s, Tinker Toys! I was very happy and proud of the fact that I had received the Tinker Toys! Out of the corner of my eye, I saw Georgie cutting across our front yard and I went to the front door and I yelled out to him "Georgie, look what I got for my birthday! Tinker Toys"! Georgie, without a second of hesitation, yelled back "You mean you got S̲tinker Toys"! Well, he laughed at his renaming of my present. I think I was a little put off by his humor! Ah, kids…

Chapter Thirty-Seven
My Final Thoughts

07/26/23

I thought that by sharing a small picture of my childhood, it might give a good example of life back then when kids were able to just be kids. Back when we were outside all day from the crack of dawn until it the street lights came on in the evening. We had so many friends from the neighborhood and school with whom we would have great adventures! I feel very fortunate to have grown up during this time and the many memories I still have. My greatest takeaway growing up during this "baby boomer" era was the ease I felt making new friends and spending time with family.

My Final Thoughts

The author saying, *"Thanks for your interest in my book"*

EPILOGUE

Years have passed and I'm now 74 years old living in Rocky River, Ohio with my wife of 44 years. My mother has since passed and so have various other family members and friends from these stories. These memories I have of growing up in Mansfield, in a great time of change, have and will forever shape who I have become.

BIOGRAPHY

John Adamescu is a retired 74 year old, living in Rocky River, Ohio with his wife, Gayle, whom he adores. They have been married for almost 44 years and have three sons and a daughter (Steve, Chris, Phil and Lizzy). John enjoys his nearly 100-year-old house, his antique automobile, and traveling, which includes trips to Hilton Head Island, Chicago, NYC, throughout the United States, and Europe. He loves a good happy hour with his wife on Fridays and a nice cigar on summer nights. Ultimately, he enjoys the time he spends with his wife, children, and grandson (Nico).

Printed in the USA
CPSIA information can be obtained
at www.ICGtesting.com
LVHW071800261023
762209LV00087B/2622